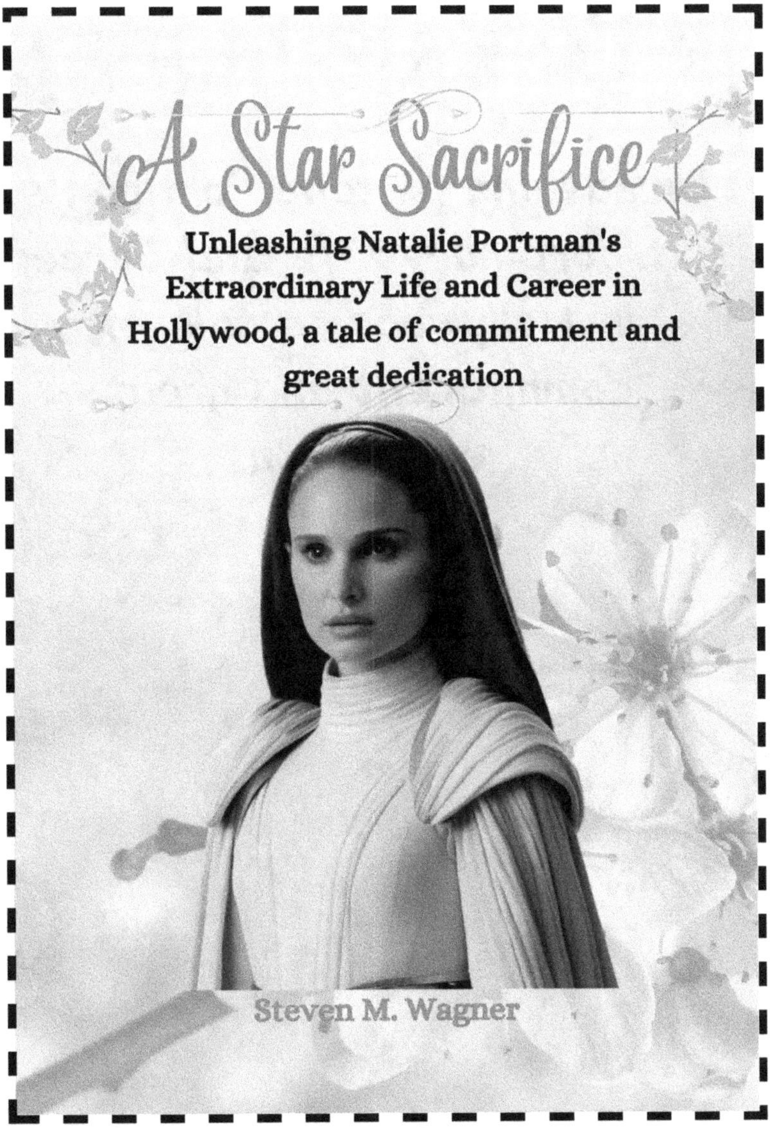

A Star Sacrifice

Unleashing Natalie Portman's Extraordinary Life and Career in Hollywood, a tale of commitment and great dedication

Steven M. Wagner

A STAR'S SACRIFICE

Unleashing Natalie Portman's Extraordinary Life and Career in Hollywood, a tale of commitment and great dedication

BY

STEVEN M. WAGNER

All rights reserved. No part of this publication may be reproduced, distributed, or transmitted in any form or by any means, including photocopying, recording, or other electronic or mechanical methods, without the prior written permission of the publisher, except in the case of brief quotations embodied in critical reviews and certain other noncommercial uses permitted by copyright law.
Copyright © Steven M. Wagner, 2024

TABLE OF CONTENTS

INTRODUCTION
CHAPTER 1
Early Years and Rise to Fame
Natalie Portman's Childhood and Ancestry
How she discovered her passion for acting
Trailblazing Roles and First Accomplishments
Moving to the United States and Adjusting to a New Culture
The Influence of Natalie Portman Parents and Her Siblings
Natalie Portman Modeling and Promotional Content at First
CHAPTER 2
Hollywood's Conquest
Natalie Portman Experienced in "Leon: The Professional"
Natalie Portman Independent Films and Transformative Roles
Appearing in the Prequels to "Star Wars"
Working Together with Prominent Directors
Natalie Portman's Impact on Fashion and Style
Natalie Portman Juggling Producing and Directing with Acting
CHAPTER 3
Getting Over Obstacles as a Young Performer

Natalie Portman Managing Adolescent Complexities in the Highlight
Natalie Portman Retaining a Normal Feeling Despite Stardom
Juggling Education with Acting Career
Managing Notoriety and Media Focus
The Value of Support Systems and Mentorship

CHAPTER 4

Intellectual Development and Academic Goals

Natalie Portman's Passion for Learning and Scientific study
Obtaining a Degree in Harvard University
The Significance of Lifelong Learning of Natalie Portman
Natalie Portman Balancing Acting and Academics Together
Promoting Education in Decent Neighborhoods

CHAPTER 5

Iconic Roles and Acting Mastery

Natalie Portman Adapting to Various Characters
Pushing Film and Performance Boundaries
The Significance of Lifelong Learning of Natalie Portman
Natalie Portman Working Together with Other Actors and Artists
The Development of Natalie Portman's Acting Style
Natalie Portman's Projects in Theater and Dancing

CHAPTER 6

Social Activism and Humanitarian Work
Natalie Portman Promoting Reproductive Health and Women's Rights
Advocating for Environmental Justifications
Advocating for the Welfare and Rights of Animals
Natalie Portman Engagement with Social and Political Issues
Promoting Civic Engagement and Voter Turnout
CHAPTER 7
Managing her Personal and Professional Lives
Natalie Portman Getting Married and Having Kids
Natalie Portman Balanced Family and Work Together
Natalie Portman Placing Value on her Well-Being and Self-Care
Handling Priorities and Time Management
Natalie Portman Helping Out Other Working Parents
CHAPTER 8
The Influence of Natalie Portman in the 21st Century
Motivating Upcoming Actors and Activist of the Next Generations
Considering Her Legacy and the Future of Her Career Development
Natalie Portman; A Classic Icon for All Time
Natalie Portman's Impact on Girls and Young Women

The Influence of Public Figures' Genuineness and Empathy

CHAPTER 9
Crafting Effective Narratives

Natalie Portman Developing Scripts and Screenwriting

Natalie Portman Character Development Process in Acting

Working Together with Directors and Screenwriters

Natalie Portman's Engagement with Short Films and Documentaries

The Storytelling Landscape in the Digital Age

CHAPTER 10
Honors, Commendations, and Appreciation

Natalie Portman's Nominations and Oscar Winnings

The Effect of Her Career's Critical Acclaim

The Value of Acknowledgment in the Entertainment Sector

Natalie Portman Giving Back via Charitable Events and Philanthropy

CHAPTER 11
The Musical Adventures of Natalie

Singing and Acting in Stage and Motion Picture Productions

Working Together with Composers and Musicians

Natalie Portman's Passion for Music and How It Affected Her Professional Life
Her Life's Intersection of Acting and Music
Discovering Novel Creative Channels and Interests
Moral Lessons from Natalie Portman's Life and Career
CONCLUSION

INTRODUCTION

Welcome to this intriguing voyage through the biography book "A Star's Sacrifice: Unleashing Natalie Portman's Extraordinary Life and Career in Hollywood, a tale of commitment and great dedication". Prepare yourself to explore the fascinating world of Natalie Portman, a remarkable lady who has impacted many lives via her humanitarian efforts and unrelenting commitment to improving the world, in addition to her success on the silver screen.

You'll be taken back in time to this gifted actress's early years as a child prodigy and her quick ascent to fame in Hollywood as you flip each page. You will learn about the difficulties she overcame, her unwavering quest for perfection, and the backstories of her well-known parts in movies such as "Leon: The Professional," "Black Swan," and the prequels to "Star Wars".

But Natalie's acting career is celebrated in this book in more ways than one. It also explores her academic record, personal life, and steadfast support of women's rights, social justice, and environmental concerns. Her narrative will captivate you, and her ardor for changing the world will touch you.

Now grab your favorite drink, settle down, and get ready to be enthralled with the remarkable story of A Star's Sacrifice: Unleashing Natalie Portman's Extraordinary Life and Career in Hollywood, a tale of commitment and great dedication, a story of immense devotion and passion. We are sure that after reading this book, you will have a deeper respect for this extraordinary lady and her amazing journey. Enjoy your reading!

CHAPTER 1

Early Years and Rise to Fame

Natalie Portman's Childhood and Ancestry

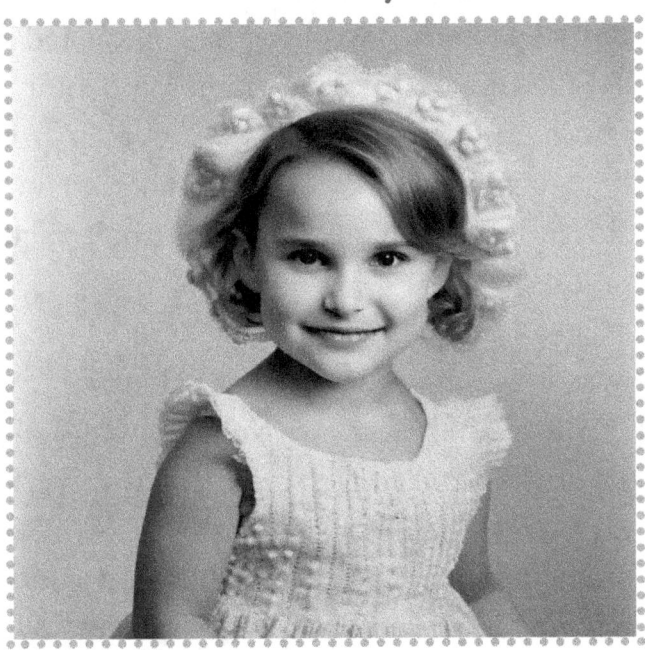

Natalie Portman in her early year

Natalie Portman a well-known actress, producer, director, and educated personnel who was born in Jerusalem, Israel, on **June 9, 1981**. She has had a significant impact on society as a whole as well as the entertainment industry. Her upbringing and family background had a significant role in shaping her into the well-known person she is today.

Her parents, Avner Hershlag and Shelley Stevens, worked in the medical field. Her father, a fertility specialist, was born in Turkey and later moved to Israel, while her mother, a doctor who was born in the United States, comes from a family with deep links to the country. The two met in Jerusalem while pursuing their medical education.

She was born into a family that valued education and professional success, so she was imbued with a strong sense of discipline and drive from an early age. Her parents instilled in her the importance of tenacity, intellectual curiosity, and acquiring knowledge. This foundation would later influence Natalie's decision to enroll at Harvard University and her lifetime passion for learning.

Natalie Portman's family immigrated to the US when she was three years old, and they lived in the suburbs of New York City. She grew up in a close-knit Jewish family that spoke Hebrew at home and celebrated both American and Israeli holidays. Because of her unique upbringing, Natalie had a strong sense of identity and respect for her cultural heritage.

Even as a little child, Natalie Portman had a natural talent for performing arts. She began taking dancing lessons when she was four years old, and she fell in love with performing right away. By the time Natalie Portman was eleven, she had already been in several local theater productions. Her parents saw her talent and encouraged her to pursue acting as a career.
During her formative years, Natalie balanced her education with her performance career. She attended many prestigious schools, including Syosset High School on Long Island, where she was an honor student and involved in extracurricular activities. Despite all of the challenges and expectations that come with

being a young actor, Natalie remained steadfast in her dedication to her studies and growth.

Also, Natalie Portman's early experiences had a big influence on her life and career. Her love of the arts, strong family values, and dedication to education have all shaped her into a well-rounded individual who never ceases to inspire others. While managing the difficulties of adolescence in the public glare, Natalie Portman remained composed and committed to her goals. Her persistence and determination had a significant role in her rise to fame and transformation into a legendary character for the twenty-first century.

How she discovered her passion for acting

Natalie Portman's early realization of the transformative power of the performing arts gave rise to her passion for acting. She would eventually transform this interest into a lifelong commitment to her work, elevating her to the status of one of the most renowned performers of her generation.

Her love of performing started to grow when she was four years old and started taking ballet courses. As she became more knowledgeable about the world of dance, she gained an appreciation for the ability to tell a story through movement and emotion. This early exposure to the performing arts aroused her curiosity and laid the foundation for her future career.

When Natalie joined the Long Island Jewish Youth Theater Group at the age of 10, her passion for acting was further piqued. She was able to hone her acting skills and try out for other roles in regional theater productions because of this opportunity. The power of narrative allowed her to transform the stage into a safe haven where she could connect with others and express herself.

As Natalie continued to improve as an actor, her parents encouraged her to pursue a career in the entertainment industry. They understood how important it was to encourage her enthusiasm while ensuring that she maintained a laser-like concentration on her studies. This balance would become a defining feature of Natalie's growth as an actress and a student.

During her teenage years, Natalie appeared in many off-Broadway plays and TV shows, including the popular serial opera "One Life to Live." These engagements aided in the advancement of her acting career and provided her with valuable experience. Notwithstanding the challenges and responsibilities that come with being a young actor, Natalie remained committed to her academics and her profession.

In 1993, Natalie's life was irrevocably changed when she was cast as Mary Mapes Dodge in the television movie adaption of "The Diary of Anne Frank." This pivotal role not only showcased Natalie's skills but also solidified her passion for acting. She gained more knowledge about the nuances of her line of work and the possible impact acting may have on audiences as a result of the experience.

Even as her acting career grew, Natalie never wavered in her belief in the importance of education. She went to many prestigious schools, such as the very tough Solomon Schechter Day School and the prestigious Syosset School. Her acting career and studies were balanced, which helped her develop a strong work ethic and multitasking skills.

In conclusion, Natalie Portman's passion for acting was discovered and nurtured at a young age. She decided to pursue an acting career while closely monitoring her academics since she has a strong interest in theater, dance, and storytelling. Events throughout her teenage years shaped her into the talented and dedicated actress she is today and laid the groundwork for her lucrative acting career.

Trailblazing Roles and First Accomplishments

It is possible to attribute Natalie Portman's early success and breakthrough roles in the entertainment industry to her innate talent, tenacity, and fortunate upbringing. Natalie's career took off after she successfully navigated the difficulties of growing up in the public eye. She was cast in many notable roles that propelled her to prominence.

In the 1994 made-for-television movie "The Diary of Anne Frank," Natalie portrayed Mary Mapes Dodge, marking one of her first noteworthy roles. This role also showcased her acting prowess and marked the start of her professional acting career. Her career was launched by the film's critical and economic success, which allowed her to explore other entrepreneurial endeavors.

In 1996, Natalie made her feature film debut in the science fiction thriller "Beautiful Girls," directed by Ted Demme. Matt Dillon, Timothy Hutton, and Uma Thurman were among the ensemble cast members in the film. Natalie's status in the entertainment industry was further cemented by the favorable reviews she received for her role in the movie.

But what actually catapulted Natalie to international fame was her breakout role in the science fiction film "Star Wars: Episode I - The Phantom Menace" in 1999. She was allowed to try out a new genre and showcase her versatility as an actress with her depiction of the young Queen Padmé Amidala. Natalie's amazing performance as the lead contributed to the movie's great box-office success, which also opened up even more professional opportunities for her.

Natalie's major break came when she starred in Mike Nichols' highly praised 2004 version of Mona Simpson's novel "Anywhere but Here." Natalie portrays Ann in the film, as a young child seeking to find her identity and negotiate the complexities of her relationship with her ambitious and eccentric mother, Susan Sarandon. This role demonstrated Natalie's ability to portray complex, adult characters, earning her a number of awards, including a

Golden Globe for Best Actress, and high appreciation from critics.

When Natalie acted in the highly acclaimed drama "Garden State," directed by Zach Braff and starring alongside him, in 2005, her career took a dramatic change. The movie further solidified her status as one of Hollywood's top actresses by showcasing her versatility on screen.

During her early years of performing, Natalie maintained a good balance between her schooling and her acting career. After attending Harvard University, she graduated with a degree in psychology. Natalie Portman's dedication to her education and her early success in the entertainment industry make her an extraordinary and inspirational figure in the performing community.

In Summary, Natalie Portman's early achievements and breakthrough roles may be attributed to her innate talent, tenacity, and fortunate upbringing. From her on-screen debut in "The Diary of Anne Frank" to her renowned performance in "Star Wars: Episode I - The Phantom Menace" and her well-regarded roles in "Anywhere but Here" and "Garden State," Natalie's early successes positioned her as a respectable and accomplished actress in the entertainment business and laid the foundation for her illustrious career.

Moving to the United States and Adjusting to a New Culture

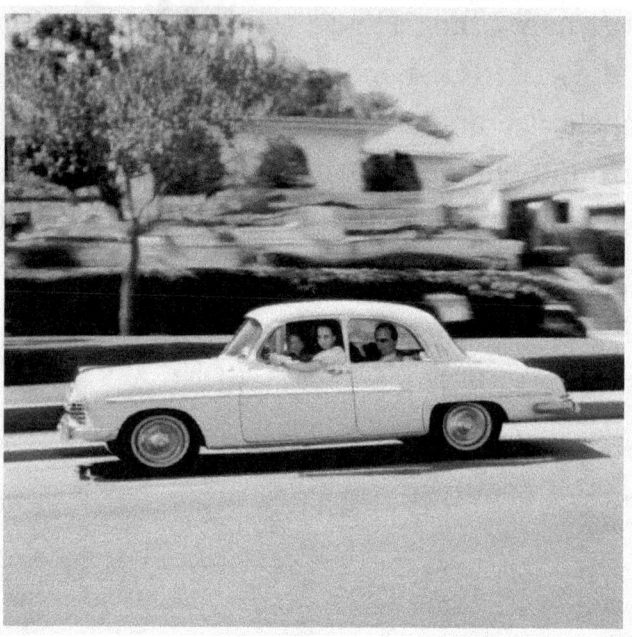

When Natalie Portman's family moved from Israel to the US in 1984, the young actress had to get used to a new language and society. This change would impact her experiences in the American entertainment industry profoundly, on an emotional and professional level.

Born in Jerusalem, Israel, Natalie Portman grew up in a family with strong Jewish roots. Her parents, Avner Hershlag and Shelley Stevens decided to move to the US to provide their children access to better educational opportunities and a safer upbringing. Natalie began the process of adjusting to a new language and culture after moving to Long Island, New York.

At first, Natalie struggled with her English, which made it difficult for her to communicate with her friends and participate in class activities. Her love of dance and the arts allowed her to express herself and communicate despite the language barrier. She would eventually discover through this dedication that she had acting talent, setting her up for success in the entertainment industry.

As Natalie began to acclimate to her new surroundings, she faced opportunities and challenges that shaped her as an actress and a person. One of her major challenges was juggling her schooling with her budding acting career. Her parents recognized the need to maintain a strict emphasis on her schooling while nurturing her love of performing, and they instilled in her a sense of responsibility and discipline that would serve her well throughout her life.

To help herself adapt to American culture, Natalie became engaged in a range of extracurricular activities, including plays at the theater and neighborhood get-togethers. She was able to improve her acting skills and learn more about the customs, beliefs, and practices of her new group via these interactions. Her desire to succeed in the performing arts was heightened as she grew to appreciate the American entertainment industry and the opportunities it offered.

During her teenage years, Natalie attended many prestigious schools, such as the Solomon Schechter Day School and then Syosset High School, to balance her academic pursuits with her performance career. She was able to develop a strong work ethic and multitasking skills via these experiences, which would be incredibly helpful in negotiating the challenges of being a young actor in the spotlight.

Natalie Portman's choice to leave Israel and relocate to the United States in 1984 was a pivotal moment in her life. Her struggles acclimating to a new language and culture ultimately shaped her experiences and contributed to her success as an actress. Natalie's love of dance and the arts provided her with a way to express herself and connect with others; this finally inspired her to follow her dream of acting. Natalie's dedication to her academics, her growing acting career, and her continuous adaptation to her new surroundings would pave the way for her extraordinary career in the US entertainment industry.

The Influence of Natalie Portman Parents and Her Siblings

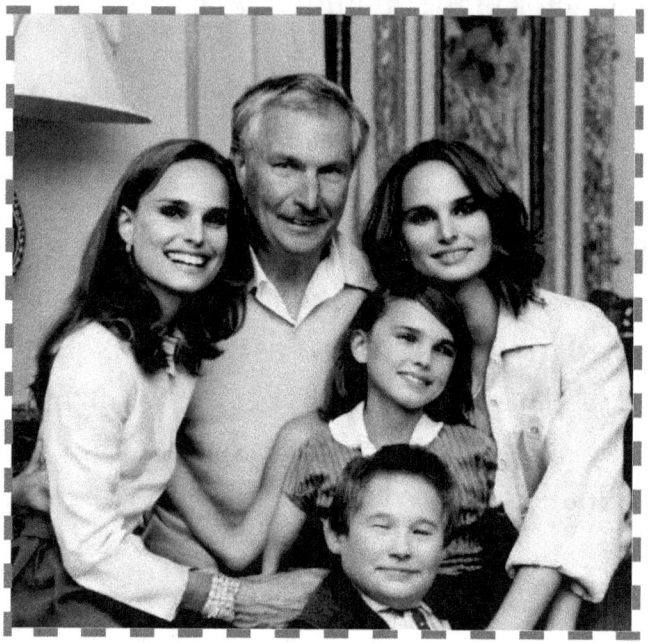

Natalie Portman, her parents and her siblings

Natalie Portman's early years and the influence of her parents and siblings have greatly influenced her present acting image. Natalie Portman was raised in a close-knit household that gave its members strong moral principles and a sense of responsibility. Avner Hershlag and Shelley Stevens are her parents.

Her father, Avner, is an Israeli reproductive physician, and her mother, Shelley, is an American artist and former journalist. Natalie had a well-rounded childhood thanks to their varied professional experiences, which exposed her to a variety of industries such as science, journalism, and the arts. This diverse experience will later in life continue to feed Natalie's curiosity and passion for learning.

Natalie Portman's two younger brothers are Avner and Gilad. Growing up with brothers, she had tight connections and a strong sense of camaraderie, which later made it easier for her to get along with co-stars and crew on film sets. Natalie's brothers also instilled in her a sense of responsibility and empathy for others, traits she would subsequently display by endorsing and championing a variety of social causes.

Natalie Portman's parents supported her in following her passion for dance and acting by allowing her to participate in after-school activities and neighborhood theater productions. This encouraging environment encouraged her to pursue her goals while maintaining a laser-like focus on her schoolwork. She would go on to become a well-known actress, activist, and scholar thanks to her parents' guidance and support.

In Summary, Natalie Portman's parents and siblings have had a significant impact on her life and career. Their guidance, support, and common values have helped her become a strong, responsible, and compassionate person. Natalie's success as an actress, scholar, and advocate for social causes has been ascribed to her exposure to a wide range of professions, as well as the importance she places on family and education. The values she learned from her family have influenced her life and career, making her a role model in the entertainment industry and beyond.

Natalie Portman Modeling and Promotional Content at First

Natalie Portman's career in entertainment began with her early modeling and commercial work. Even before she started performing, professionals in the industry were captivated by Natalie's extraordinary beauty and natural charm, which inspired her to explore modeling and business opportunities.

When Natalie was ten years old, she appeared in her first commercial for a chocolate pudding dessert called "Neverfull." While appearing in this commercial provided her a taste of show business, it also gave her confidence when she was on camera.

Her passion for modeling and acting expanded, and she began working with several agencies and photographers. She eventually joined the esteemed Ford Models agency, and for many years, they acted as her agent, exhibiting her natural beauty and adaptability in a plethora of print advertisements and catalogs.

The most well-known early modeling role Natalie had was for the Israeli company "Fair Lady," where she featured in national commercials and billboards. This helped Natalie become well-known in her own land and laid the groundwork for her later acting career.

She featured in many music videos in the early years of her career in addition to working in print and commercial advertisements. Her first public appearance was in the 1996 music video for the song "Beautiful" by American singer Sinead O'Connor. The following year, she gained additional experience performing in front of the camera when she made a cameo in Madonna's "Crazy for You" music video.

Throughout her early modeling and advertising career, Natalie continued to hone her skills and fortify her work ethic. This not only prepared the way for her acting career but also provided priceless insights into professionalism, self-assurance, and teamwork.

To sum up, Natalie Portman's success as an actor was greatly influenced by her early work in modeling and advertising. It improved her confidence in front of the camera, sharpened her abilities, and set the foundation for her future in show business. Natalie used the skills and understanding from her early modeling career to her acting career, which eventually helped her succeed in Hollywood and other places.

CHAPTER 2

Hollywood's Conquest

Natalie Portman Experienced in "Leon: The Professional"

Natalie Portman's breakthrough performance in the 1994 motion picture "Leon: The Professional" established her as a gifted and promising young actress and served as a turning point in her career. This action movie, which was directed by Luc Besson and starred Jean Reno as well, followed the tale of a little girl called Matilda who befriends a professional assassin named Leon despite their differences.

Natalie Portman, who was just 12 years old at the time, was well-recognized and received critical praise for her portrayal of Mathilda in the movie. The popularity of the movie was mostly due to Natalie's portrayal of a sophisticated, sensitive, and mature heroine for her age.

Furthermore, she went through a rigorous training program to be ready for the part, which included learning how to wield a gun correctly, picking pockets, and speaking with a French accent. Even at such a young age, her devotion to providing authenticity and depth to her character was shown by her dedication to her profession.

Natalie Portman's first significant part in a feature film, "Leon: The Professional" gave her exposure to a larger audience domestically and abroad. Her career took off thanks to the film's popularity, which also made it possible for her to take on more difficult parts in the future.
Working on "Leon: The Professional" gave Natalie Moore vital insight into the filmmaking process and the value of teamwork. Working with seasoned pros like Jean Reno and Luc Besson gave her the chance to learn from and be guided by their knowledge and experience. Her development as an actor and her readiness for the several projects that would come after was greatly influenced by this mentoring.

In addition, Natalie was able to experiment with a variety of roles and genres across her career due to the critical and financial success of "Leon: The Professional". Natalie's flexibility as an actress—which spans genres from drama and romance to science fiction and fantasy—can be attributed to the foundation she laid while working on this ground-breaking movie.

To sum up, Natalie Portman's time spent on "Leon: The Professional" was a pivotal point in her professional life. The movie gave her the chance to learn from seasoned pros and hone her acting abilities in addition to showcasing her extraordinary gift. She was able to take on more difficult projects and solidify her reputation as a formidable force in the entertainment business thanks to her breakthrough performance.

Natalie Portman Independent Films and Transformative Roles

Natalie Portman has shown her flexibility as an actor and her commitment to delving into intricate and thought-provoking characters by persistently pursuing transformational parts in indie films. She has been able to explore the human condition more deeply thanks to these independent cinema projects, often assuming characters that go against social norms and traditional narrative conventions.

The dystopian thriller "V for Vendetta" (2005), which is set in a future totalitarian society, features Natalie as Evey Hammond, one of her most well-known independent cinema performances. Natalie's character in this movie experiences a dramatic change in both her physical and mental makeup as she joins a revolt against the repressive regime. The film's themes of resistance, power, and independence struck a chord with viewers and cemented Natalie's place as one of the top actresses in the indie cinema industry.

Natalie Portman had the lead role in Mike Nichols' drama "Closer," which delves into the intricacies of contemporary relationships and the influence of technology on interpersonal bonds, and was directed in 2006. Natalie, who played a stripper-turned-actress called Alice, won a Golden Globe and was nominated for an Academy Award for Best Actress for her compelling and nuanced portrayal. As Alice navigates her relationships with three other characters, each of whom has secrets and agendas of their own, this part demonstrates her ability to represent a character with several dimensions.

She had another pivotal performance in Darren Aronofsky's psychological thriller "Black Swan" (2010). She portrayed Nina in this movie, a gifted but emotionally frail ballet dancer who battles to maintain her composure and perfection while vying for the lead part in Tchaikovsky's Swan Lake. Natalie became even more well-known as a powerful actress in the independent cinema industry when her work in

"Black Swan" won her several awards, including the Academy Award for Best Actress.

Also, her portrayal of former First Lady Jacqueline Kennedy in the historical drama "Jackie" (2016) demonstrated her continuous dedication to indie cinema ventures. Natalie had to become proficient in her American accent to play this part and effectively convey the dignity, composure, and sorrow of a historical character. Her portrayal in "Jackie" garnered her praise from critics and led to nominations for the Academy Award and the Golden Globes for Best Actress.

Natalie Portman's remarkable acting skills have been highlighted by these pivotal parts in independent films, which have also given her the chance to explore a variety of nuanced and thought-provoking characters. She has become a renowned and admired figure in the indie film industry by accepting these difficult parts since they show her commitment to the craft of acting and her willingness to go outside of her comfort zone.

Appearing in the Prequels to "Star Wars"

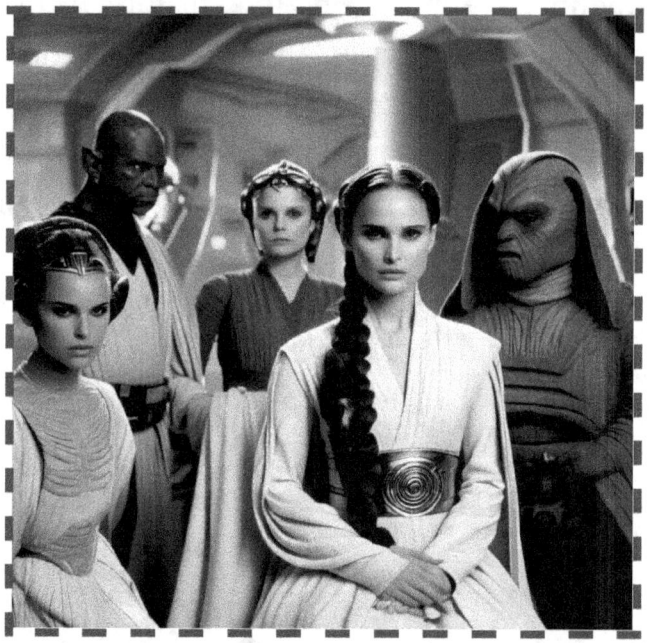

Natalie Portman acting as "Padmé Amidala" in the "Star Wars"

An important turning point in Natalie Portman's acting career came when she played the legendary character of Padmé Amidala in the "Star Wars" prequel trilogy. Amidala is a political figure who eventually becomes the protagonist Anakin Skywalker's love interest.

Natalie was able to expand her audience and solidify her reputation in the film industry by playing this role in the much-awaited movies.

Set decades before the events of the original "Star Wars" trilogy, the prequel trilogy features three films: "The Phantom Menace" (1999), "Attack of the Clones" (2002), and "Revenge of the Sith" (2005). It centers on the rise of the Galactic Empire and the transformation of Anakin Skywalker into the notorious Darth Vader. Padmé Amidala, portrayed by Natalie, was a significant player in the galactic political scene. She held the position of senator and subsequently wed Anakin Skywalker in secret.

Natalie Portman researched political speeches and worked hard to polish her character's distinctive makeup and outfit in preparation for the part. Before playing a senator in the later movies, she also had to learn how to play a young queen in "The Phantom Menace" with conviction. Natalie Portman's portrayal of Padmé Amidala in the prequel trilogy demonstrated her capacity to portray both the emotional depth needed for a prominent part in a major film series and the strength and determination of the character.

Despite the mixed reviews for the prequel trilogy, reviewers and fans alike praised Natalie Portman's portrayal of Padmé Amidala. She was able to explore a new aspect of her acting repertoire by delving into the world of science fiction and fantasy via her depiction of the character. Her participation in the "Star Wars" film series also allowed her to collaborate with several well-known actors, such as Hayden Christensen and Ewan McGregor, who portrayed her romantic interest in the film.

Natalie Portman's career was greatly impacted by the "Star Wars" prequel trilogy, which solidified her position as a top actress in the entertainment business and brought her to a broader audience. She was also able to hone her acting abilities while working on these movies, which helped her get ready for all the other roles she would play in the years to come.

Ultimately, Natalie Portman's role in the "Star Wars" prequel trilogy proved to be a crucial turning point in her acting career. She was able to showcase her versatility in various roles and genres and reach a wider audience by starring in these eagerly awaited movies. Natalie's portrayal of Padmé Amidala was largely well-received, even though the prequel trilogy's reception was not entirely favorable. This helped to sustain Natalie's success in the movie industry.

Working Together with Prominent Directors

Natalie Portman has collaborated with several eminent directors. Through these partnerships, she has been able to develop her craft and leave a lasting impression on the film industry in addition to exploring a variety of roles.

Her first working relationship with a well-known director was in "The Professional," a 1994 movie in which Luc Besson cast her as a young child named Matilda. Natalie had the chance to demonstrate her acting abilities at an early age thanks to Besson's distinctive visual aesthetic and storytelling methods.

Natalie Portman collaborated with Mike Nichols on the 1999 adaptation of the Pulitzer Prize–winning play "Closer," in which she starred with Clive Owen, Julia Roberts, and Jude Law. Natalie was able to give her character, Alice, a woman navigating the complexities of love and relationships in contemporary society, more depth and complexity thanks to Nichols' directing.

Another noteworthy partnership was with director Darren Aronofsky on the 2010 psychological thriller "Black Swan." Aronofsky's demanding and methodical approach forced Natalie to the brink of her abilities, leading to a compelling and Academy Award–winning portrayal as Nina, a ballet dancer battling her inner demons and the pressure to perform flawlessly.

In the 2015 biographical drama "Jackie," Natalie collaborated with Pablo Larraín, portraying former First Lady Jacqueline Kennedy. Natalie was able to delve into the deep feelings and inner turmoil of a historical figure thanks to Larraín's distinctive storytelling style, which produced a performance that was highly praised.

Natalie Portman most recently worked with Marielle Heller on the 2019 film "A Beautiful Day in the Neighborhood," in which she portrayed Matthew Rhys's wife, Andrea Vogel, a journalist. Heller's empathic and caring directing helped Natalie build a multidimensional character that brought depth to the film's theme of empathy and healing.

These partnerships with famous filmmakers have not only boosted Natalie Portman's acting career but have also helped her to mature as an artist. By working with a vast spectrum of directors, she has been able to explore many genres and play a wide assortment of characters, further confirming her image as a skilled and flexible actor in the film business.

Natalie Portman's Impact on Fashion and Style

Natalie Portman's effect on fashion and style goes beyond her playing profession, as she has continually shown her distinct sense of fashion and style at numerous events, red carpets, and film premieres. Her dress choices have developed throughout the years, expressing her development and maturity while also defining trends and influencing others.

From her early days in Hollywood, Natalie was already making a statement with her dress choices. She generally chose modest, beautiful clothes that accentuated her inherent beauty and subtle splendor. This attitude to fashion connected with many, as it displayed a sense of self-confidence and taste that was both timeless and current.

As Natalie's career evolved, so did her wardrobe choices. She started experimenting with bolder and more adventurous trends, frequently infusing themes of sustainability and eco-friendliness into her clothing. This devotion to sustainable design was clear when she donned a gown made from recycled plastic bottles to the 2019 Academy Awards, bringing awareness about environmental concerns while looking magnificent.

Her affinity for fashion has also led her to partner with many designers and businesses. In 2008, she became the face of Dior's Miss Dior Cherie campaign, further establishing her standing as a fashion star. She has also collaborated with Rodarte, a fashion firm noted for its avant-garde creations, for the 2010 Oscars, donning a custom-made gown that gained considerable appreciation for its unusual look.

Along with her work with well-known designers, Natalie has pushed for the backing of small fashion businesses and emerging designers. She has helped raise awareness for these designers and aided in their success by wearing their pieces on the red carpet and at prestigious events.

Natalie Portman's influence on style and fashion extends beyond her preferences; she has also advocated for changes in the fashion industry via her platform. As a vegan, she has advocated for customers and designers to embrace more sustainable and cruelty-free methods by speaking out against the usage of animal products in apparel and accessories.

Finally, Natalie Portman's impact on fashion and style may be attributed to her distinct sense of personal style, her openness to trying out new looks, her dedication to sustainability, and her support of up-and-coming designers. Her choices in clothing have changed over the years, reflecting both her personal and professional development as an actor and her desire to encourage people to value their uniqueness and make thoughtful fashion decisions.

Natalie Portman Juggling Producing and Directing with Acting

In addition to her success as an actor, Natalie Portman has shown herself as a filmmaker and producer. In the film business, juggling this many responsibilities calls for a high level of commitment, time management skills, and love for the work. Natalie's career has been enhanced by her ability to manage these many tasks, which has also enabled her to make a substantial contribution to the film business in several ways. As an actor, Natalie has been in several highly regarded movies that highlight her skill and adaptability. She has investigated producing and directing, yet her passion for the filmmaking process goes beyond performing. She was a co-founder of Handsomecharlie Films, a production business that specializes in making entertaining and thought-provoking media, in 2004. With this business, Natalie has produced several films, including "A Tale of Love and Darkness," "The Death and Life of John F. Donovan," and "Eve," which she also directed.

Natalie Portman proved she could tell a compelling narrative behind the camera with her feature debut, "A Tale of Love and Darkness" (2015). Based on Amos Oz's autobiographical book, the movie gave Natalie the chance to demonstrate her narrative skills and her capacity to empathize with the character's feelings. Even though the movie had mixed reviews, Natalie's career as a filmmaker and her dedication to producing important tales began with it.

Natalie Portman continues to perform in a variety of projects in addition to her work as a producer and director, demonstrating her commitment to the field. She has been picky about the parts she takes on, choosing ones that push her creative boundaries and let her investigate various facets of the human condition. Her ability to strike a balance between directing, producing, and acting has helped her develop as an artist and make several contributions to the cinema business.

As a producer, Natalie has worked on films like "Annihilation" (2018) and "Vox Lux" (2018) that raise awareness of social and environmental issues. These movies not only show off her ability to produce thought-provoking material but also her devotion to utilizing her platform to raise awareness of crucial causes.

It takes a huge lot of enthusiasm, time management, and effort to balance performing, producing, and directing. Natalie Portman's ability to handle these many obligations well is evidence of her dedication to the film business and her willingness to work in it in a variety of ways. Natalie will surely continue to have a huge and inspirational influence on the film industry as she develops as an artist.

CHAPTER 3

Getting Over Obstacles as a Young Performer

Natalie Portman Managing Adolescent Complexities in the Highlight

Anyone must navigate adolescence, but it gets significantly more difficult when they have to deal with the demands and attention that come with being a star. Natalie Portman's experience growing up in the spotlight provides insightful information on how she struck a careful balance and went on to become a great actor and person.

Natalie Portman's acting career got its start when she was only 12 years old, landing her first part in "Leon: The Professional" (1994). She shot to fame after her early triumph, becoming a well-known figure in Hollywood very soon. Natalie's youth was thus characterized by the particular difficulties that accompany being a child celebrity.

Keeping her normality in the face of continual public attention was one of the biggest hurdles Natalie had to overcome as a teenager. She has often mentioned in interviews how important it was to have a loving family and close friends who kept her grounded throughout this difficult period. Natalie's mother, in particular, was instrumental in making sure that her education always came first, and she attended normal schools in addition to her acting duties.

During her teens, Natalie also had to contend with the expectations put on young actors in the entertainment business and the pressure to live up to society's ideals of beauty. Natalie has been transparent about her challenges with self-esteem and the influence of how women's bodies are portrayed in the media at a time when body image concerns are common. Many people have found resonance in this candor because it emphasizes the need for self-acceptance and body positivity, particularly for young females navigating their adolescence.

Although being a child celebrity came with its own set of difficulties, Natalie Portman's youth was distinguished by her devotion to her work and her determination to use her platform for good. She persisted in accepting difficult parts that enabled her to explore different facets of the human experience and displayed her acting talent. She also started engaging in activism and charity, using her notoriety to advocate for causes like environmental preservation, animal welfare, and women's rights.

Finally, it can be said that Natalie Portman's public adolescence was a complicated experience. Her courage, resiliency, and determination are shown by her ability to overcome these challenges while retaining her love of acting and her resolve to change the world. Natalie's story inspires young people going through comparable difficulties by emphasizing the value of being true to oneself and utilizing one's platform for the benefit of society.

Natalie Portman Retaining a Normal Feeling Despite Stardom

Any celebrity who wants to remain normal in the face of continual public attention and entertainment business expectations must overcome these obstacles to maintain their feeling of normalcy. Natalie Portman's strategy for striking a balance between her work and personal life provides insightful information on how she has maintained her composure throughout her public persona.

Her solid support network of family members is one of the primary reasons Natalie has been able to keep her sense of normalcy in the face of fame. Natalie's mother, in particular, has been instrumental in keeping her upbringing as similar to a typical childhood as possible. They put her education first, letting her balance her acting responsibilities with normal schooling. Natalie's ability to stay grounded in real-world situations has allowed her to be aware of the world outside of the glitz and glamor of Hollywood.

Her selection of responsibilities and tasks is a crucial component of her strategy for preserving normalcy. She has made deliberate decisions throughout her career, choosing parts that push her creatively and provide her the chance to investigate many facets of the human condition. Natalie has been able to retain a feeling of satisfaction and purpose in her job by concentrating on interesting and relevant initiatives, which in turn helps her remain anchored in reality.

Natalie Portman's capacity to retain her sense of normalcy in the face of fame is also greatly influenced by her commitment to her studies and intellectual interests. She studied psychology at Harvard University, where she also received her degree. Throughout her life, she has remained interested in academic and intellectual subjects. She has been able to keep connected to the world outside of the entertainment business because of her devotion to learning and personal development, which has helped her stay grounded and well-rounded.

In addition, Natalie Portman's activism and charitable contributions have been crucial to her attempts to keep her normalcy in the face of fame. Through her platform, Natalie has been able to concentrate on topics that go beyond her personal and professional life, such as animal welfare, environmental protection, and women's rights. Her determination to change the world for the better has given her a feeling of contentment and purpose, which has further helped her to preserve her normalcy in the face of fame.

In summary, Natalie Portman's steadfast familial support network, deliberate job choices, commitment to learning and intellectual endeavors, and engagement in activism and charity all contribute to her capacity to retain her sense of normalcy in the face of celebrity. These elements have made her a resilient figure for those negotiating the difficulties of fame and popularity, enabling her to maintain her sense of self and connection to the world beyond the entertainment business.

Juggling Education with Acting Career

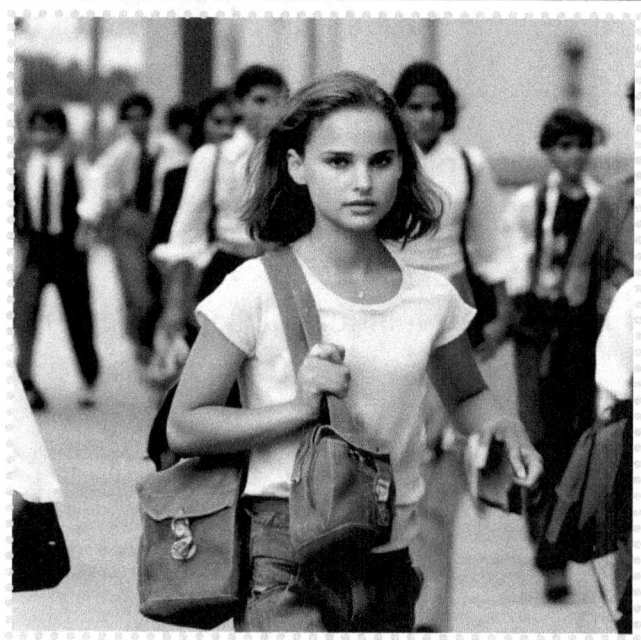

Natalie Portman during her studying at age 12

Anyone might find it difficult to juggle school with an acting career, but Natalie Portman, a young actress thrown into the spotlight, may find it particularly difficult. But Natalie's resolve to put her studies first even while she pursues her acting career is evidence of her fortitude and dedication to self-improvement.

After obtaining her breakthrough part in "Leon: The Professional" (1994), Natalie started juggling her acting career with school at the age of twelve. Natalie's parents insisted that she complete her academics in addition to her acting responsibilities, despite the unexpected attention and popularity that came with her recent success. This focus on education set the stage for Natalie's lifelong commitment to study and personal development.

Natalie Portman often worked with tutors on site or during pauses in production to accommodate her education. This made it possible for her to continue her education and pursue her acting profession at the same time. She also went to conventional schools, which gave her a feeling of normality and made it possible for her to socialize with her classmates outside of the entertainment sector.

She made a big educational leap in 1999 when she enrolled at Harvard University. She postponed her admission for a year to work on the movie "Anywhere but Here" (1999), but she ultimately enrolled in the esteemed school. Natalie's pursuit of a psychology degree at Harvard demonstrated her dedication to learning and her ambition to comprehend human experience outside of the performing arts.

She had difficulties between her acting career and her studies. She had to be a skilled time manager since she often had to balance hard academic obligations with tight filming commitments. However, she was able to succeed in both fields because of her commitment to her studies and acting career.

Natalie Portman's life and career have been significantly impacted by her ability to juggle her acting profession with academics. Her solid educational background has given her the ability to approach her jobs with a greater comprehension of human behavior and emotions. Her dedication to education has also stoked her interest and enthusiasm for using acting to explore a variety of facets of the human experience.

In summary, Natalie Portman's story of juggling education with a career in acting is a brilliant illustration of how one may follow their hobbies while placing a high value on education and personal development. She is an inspiration to students and aspiring actors alike because of her unwavering commitment to maintaining a solid educational foundation, which has enhanced her acting career and enabled her to make significant contributions to several sectors.

Managing Notoriety and Media Focus

Anyone who finds themselves in the spotlight at an early age, like Natalie Portman, knows how difficult it can be to deal with celebrity and media attention. Natalie has shown that she can protect her private and mental health in the face of continual scrutiny by navigating this environment with elegance, resiliency, and a strong sense of self.

Natalie Portman has a great support network, which is one of the main reasons she can handle her notoriety and media attention. Her mother in particular has been instrumental in providing her with a feeling of stability and normality throughout her childhood. Her capacity to deal with the difficulties of celebrity has been greatly aided by their instillation in her of the significance of family values, education, and being true to herself.

Additionally, Natalie Portman has exercised discretion in the projects and public appearances she chooses, making sure that she only takes part in endeavors that are consistent with her principles and worldview. She has been able to manage her public image and preserve some privacy thanks to her selectiveness, which has also helped her deal with the continuous attention from the media.

Natalie Portman uses her dedication to her hobbies and personal life outside of the entertainment business as another crucial coping strategy. She has continued to study academic and intellectual subjects and has graduated from Harvard University with a degree in psychology. Her commitment to education and self-improvement has given her a sense of direction and satisfaction that extends beyond her acting profession, enabling her to lead a balanced life despite the pressures of celebrity.

Furthermore, a big component of Natalie Portman's coping mechanism has been her activism and charity. Through her platform, Natalie has been able to concentrate on topics that go beyond her personal and professional life, such as animal welfare, environmental protection, and women's rights. Her determination to change the world has given her a feeling of satisfaction and purpose, which has further aided in her capacity to handle the pressures of notoriety and media attention.

Finally, Natalie Portman's modesty and self-awareness might be credited for her ability to handle celebrity and media attention. She has been able to establish a closer connection with her followers by being transparent about her battles with anxiety and body image. Natalie has shown that, despite her famous position, she is a real person by opening up about her insecurities.

In conclusion, Natalie Portman's resilience to celebrity and media attention may be attributed to a number of factors, including her robust support network, deliberate decision-making when taking on projects and making public appearances, dedication to her personal life and hobbies, activism and charitable work, humility, and self-awareness. She is an inspirational role model for people navigating the difficulties of celebrity since these elements have helped her to preserve her privacy, mental health, and sense of self despite the continual scrutiny that comes with being a public person.

The Value of Support Systems and Mentorship

Individuals' personal and professional development is greatly aided by mentorship and support networks, particularly in the very demanding and competitive entertainment industry. The path taken by Natalie Portman demonstrates the value of support networks and mentoring in influencing her professional and personal development.

Natalie Portman's parents were her first source of support from a young age, teaching her the importance of perseverance, hard effort, and self-truth. They supported her in following her interests while keeping a solid academic foundation, which ultimately affected her choice to enroll at Harvard University. Natalie's lifelong dedication to lifelong learning and self-improvement was made possible by this early focus on education and personal development.

She has had the good fortune to work with mentors in the entertainment business who have helped her refine her skills and deal with the demands of celebrity. Director Luc Besson is one such mentor; the two worked together on "The Professional" (1994) and "Léon: The

Professional" (1994). He saw her promise early on and gave her invaluable advice and encouragement, which helped her hone her acting abilities and deal with the challenges of the movie business.

Natalie Portman has also asked her classmates and business colleagues for advice. Actors Scarlett Johansson and Jake Gyllenhaal are among the close relationships she has made with other actors who have helped her throughout her career. These connections have given her possibilities for development and learning as well as emotional support by sharing their experiences and ideas from their own travels in the entertainment industry.

Also, she has a network of personal supporters in addition to her involvement in several activist and humanitarian endeavors, where she has been inspired and mentored by people who are dedicated to improving society. Her network of like-minded people has backed her in her efforts to bring about good change, thanks to organizations like the Vegan Animal Charity

Evaluators and the Women's Media Center, which she co-founded.

Moreover, Natalie's dedication to learning beyond her scholastic endeavors. She has supported programs designed to provide children from different backgrounds similar chances and has been an advocate for educational reform. Natalie has not only improved society by helping the next generation of learners and mentoring them, but she has also benefited from the inspiration and drive of the bright young people she has had the opportunity to work with.

To sum up, Natalie Portman's personal and professional development has been greatly aided by mentoring and support networks. From her parents and early teachers to her coworkers in the entertainment sector and her participation in charitable and activist endeavors, Natalie has been surrounded by people who have offered her direction, consolation, and emotional support. She credits these mentorships and support networks with helping to shape her character, profession, and dedication to changing the world for the better.

CHAPTER 4

Intellectual Development and Academic Goals

Natalie Portman's Passion for Learning and Scientific study

Natalie Portman's passion for science and learning is evidence of her complex nature, as well as her commitment to intellectual inquiry and personal development. She has shown a lifelong interest in a variety of scientific fields and has pushed herself to further her studies.

In her early years, Natalie's parents encouraged her to follow her interests and keep a solid academic foundation, which is one of the first signs of her enthusiasm for science and education. Her mother, a professor of Jewish studies, taught her the value of education and scholastic curiosity. Natalie's passion for science and dedication to study were shaped by her background.

She did well academically as a student, earning her admission to Harvard University and a psychology degree there. Her study on the effects of stress on the brain was motivated by her interest in the topic, and in 2003 she gave a presentation on it at a conference. Her commitment to scientific investigation and her desire to further psychology were shown by this event.

Natalie has shown interest in several different scientific fields, demonstrating her passion for research beyond psychology. She has spoken about how astronomy fascinates her and she has gone to events about space travel and the hunt for alien life. She has also shown an interest in environmental science, gone vegan, and become an advocate for environmental preservation and animal welfare.

A supporter of educational reform, Natalie also has a particular interest in science. She has backed programs that provide children from all backgrounds with similar chances because she thinks that education is a basic right that can strengthen communities and people. Her dedication to the value of education is further shown by her participation in groups like the Genesis Prize Foundation, which promotes Jewish creativity and education.

Natalie's passion for education and science is shown in her acting profession as well. She has played actual scientists and mathematicians in movies like "Black Swan" (2010) and "Pi" (1998), demonstrating her commitment to faithfully portraying these professions on screen. These jobs have allowed her to further explore the fields of science and academics in addition to showcasing her acting abilities.

In summary, Natalie Portman's passion for science and learning has shaped her life and profession. Natalie has shown to be a great believer in intellectual curiosity and personal development through her academic endeavors, participation in educational reform, and representation of scientific characters in motion pictures. Her enthusiasm for these topics not only improves her life but also encourages others to learn about and value education and the marvels of science.

Obtaining a Degree in Harvard University

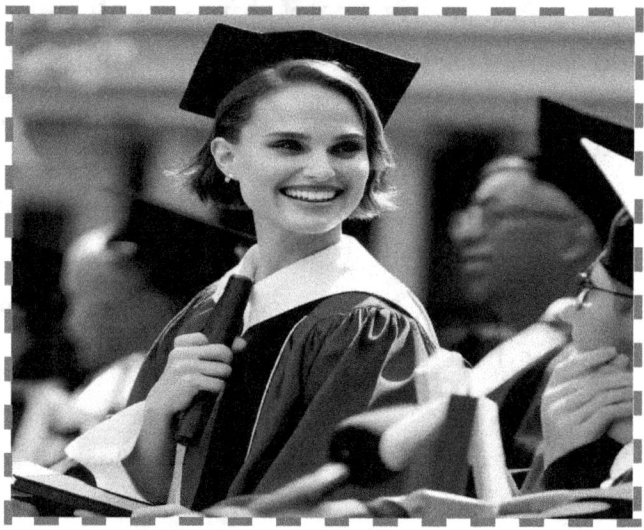

Natalie Portman's Harvard University degree is evidence of her commitment to learning and her inquisitiveness. She demonstrated her attention and perseverance by managing to juggle her academic obligations and earning a psychology degree while pursuing a successful acting career.

After putting her education first and taking a vacation from acting, Natalie started her adventure at Harvard University in 1999. She planned to get a degree in psychology at the renowned university since the field had always captivated her. Natalie persevered in her academic pursuits despite the difficulties she faced juggling her growing acting career with her education.

Natalie maintained her acting career while attending Harvard, appearing in movies including "Where the Heart Is" (1999), "Anywhere but Here" (1999), and "Thor" (2011) while balancing her studies. She proved throughout her stay at the university that she had excellent time management, discipline, and attention.

Natalie studied the effects of stress on the brain in addition to her schoolwork, and in 2003 she gave a presentation on the subject at a conference. This encounter demonstrated her commitment to scientific investigation and her desire to further psychology even in the course of her performing profession.

Natalie earned a bachelor's degree in psychology from Harvard University in 2003. Her graduation proved to be a noteworthy accomplishment in her life, proving that she could succeed in both the entertainment and academic domains. Others were inspired by this achievement, especially young women, who may have been debating between prioritizing their studies and following their hobbies.

Natalie has always shown her passion for science and education throughout her career. She has been an advocate for school reform and has supported programs that try to provide children from all backgrounds similar chances. Her life, both on and off screen, has consistently revolved around her dedication to study and personal development.

In conclusion, Natalie Portman's Harvard University graduation is an incredible accomplishment that demonstrates her commitment to learning and inquisitiveness. She balanced her academic obligations with the pressures of her acting job and eventually graduated with a psychology degree. This achievement highlights the value of following one's interests while maintaining a solid educational foundation and inspiring others in the process.

The Significance of Lifelong Learning of Natalie Portman

Natalie Portman places a high value on lifelong learning, which is indicative of her dedication to intellectual curiosity, personal development, and information acquisition. She has continuously shown throughout her career that she is passionate about learning in a variety of subjects, such as science, education, and the arts. Natalie's passion for learning started early in life when her parents encouraged her to pursue a variety of interests and keep up a solid academic foundation. She learned the importance of lifelong learning and the quest for knowledge from her childhood.

The choice Natalie made to enroll at Harvard University after being a well-known actress is among the most noteworthy instances of her commitment to continued study. She put her acting career on hold to concentrate on her education, and in 2003 she graduated with a bachelor's degree in psychology. This experience demonstrated her dedication to education and her readiness to push herself intellectually despite the pressures of her acting profession.

She has shown to have a desire to learn in a variety of subjects outside of academia. She has shown an interest in mathematics, astronomy, and environmental science by going to events and conversing with professionals in these fields. The traits of a lifelong learner are her curiosity and willingness to broaden her knowledge base.
Also, her acting career demonstrates her dedication to continual learning. She has played actual scientists and mathematicians in movies like "Black Swan" (2010) and "Pi" (1998), demonstrating her commitment to faithfully

portraying these professions on screen. Her acting career has been enhanced by these jobs, which have also allowed her to learn more about education and science.

She has also supported efforts to provide pupils from all backgrounds similar chances in school and has been a champion for educational reform. Her engagement with organizations like the Genesis Prize Foundation, which promotes Jewish education and creativity, shows her dedication to the value of lifelong learning. She thinks that education is a basic right that can empower people and communities.

Natalie Portman's commitment to intellectual curiosity, personal development, and the quest for knowledge is shown by the significance of lifelong learning in her life. Her dedication to lifelong learning, her accomplishments in the classroom, and her support of educational reform all serve as role models for those who see the need for lifelong learning. Natalie's story demonstrates the transformational potential of lifelong learning for people and society at large.

Natalie Portman Balancing Acting and Academics Together

Natalie Portman's commitment, attention, and time management abilities are evident in her ability to balance her scholastic endeavors and acting career. She has shown a lifelong dedication to the arts and academics, demonstrating the possibility for people to achieve success in many areas at once.

Her career started when she was young and began acting, making appearances in several TV series and movies that won her praise from critics and a devoted following. She had early success in the entertainment business, but she never wavered in her dedication to learning, keeping a solid academic foundation throughout her adolescence.

Also, she decided to put her acting career on hold in 1999 to concentrate on her studies at Harvard University, where she was pursuing a psychology degree. This choice demonstrated her commitment to education and her willingness to delve deeply into scholarly issues. Natalie maintained her acting career while attending Harvard, appearing in movies including "Where the Heart Is" (1999), "Anywhere but Here" (1999), and "Thor" (2011), showcasing her capacity to manage both her acting and academic obligations.

She had to prioritize her academic and acting responsibilities to acquire extraordinary time management abilities. She would often take time off from her studies to work on movie sets, making sure that her performance in class remained unaffected. She would also set aside time for homework and study, making sure that her academic goals always came first.

Furthermore, Natalie's commitment to her studies and acting carried over into her personal life. She carried out studies on the effects of stress on the brain when she was a Harvard student, and in 2003 she gave a presentation on her results. This event demonstrated her love of science and her ambition to advance psychology even while she pursued her acting career.

Natalie kept fusing her passions for performing and academia after earning a bachelor's degree in psychology from Harvard University in 2003. In movies like "Pi" (1998) and "Black Swan" (2010), she has played real-life scientists and mathematicians, demonstrating her dedication to faithfully portraying these professions on screen. Her acting career has been enhanced by these jobs, which have also allowed her to learn more about education and science.

In conclusion, Natalie Portman's accomplishment of fusing performance with academics is noteworthy and demonstrates her commitment, concentration, and extraordinary time management abilities. She has shown throughout her life that people may be successful in many different sectors at the same time, encouraging others to follow their interests while still having a solid educational foundation. Natalie's story offers a compelling illustration of how to effectively traverse the nexus between the arts and academics, enhancing one's development on the personal and professional levels.

Promoting Education in Decent Neighborhoods

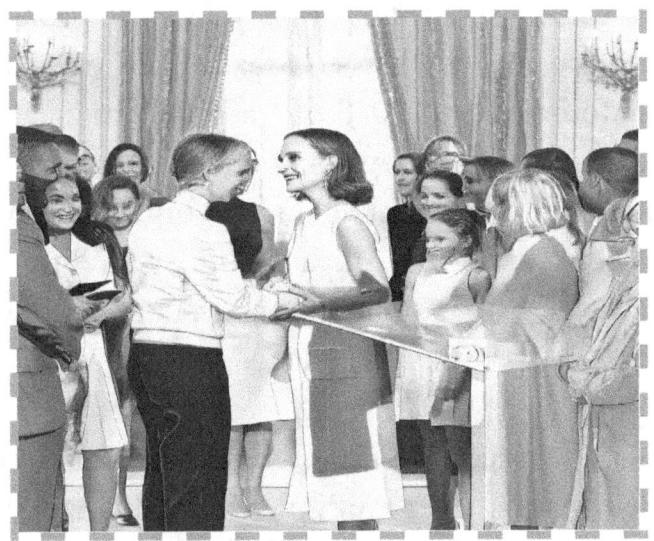

Natalie Portman while receiving Genesis Prize in 2018

Natalie Portman's dedication to learning surpasses her scholastic accomplishments. She has been a proponent of educational reform, especially in impoverished areas where there is often restricted access to high-quality education.

Natalie Portman has devoted her life to advancing equitable opportunities for kids from a variety of backgrounds because she firmly believes that education is a basic right that can empower both people and communities.

Her work with the Genesis Prize Foundation is among her most noteworthy contributions to education in underserved areas. The Foundation was founded in 2013 to advance education, innovation, and Jewish values. Natalie has shown her commitment to the organization by actively supporting it and understanding the significance of maintaining and fostering Jewish culture, identity, and values.

Also, she received the Genesis Prize in 2018, which entails a $1 million reward that may be given to any charity of the winner's choosing. Natalie decided to donate the money to several groups that support Jewish innovation and education. This choice demonstrates her commitment to using her wealth and influence to improve the educational landscape.

Natalie Portman has backed several projects targeted at giving kids from different backgrounds equitable chances in addition to her work with the Genesis Prize Foundation. She has been active in groups like the American Civil Freedoms Union (ACLU), which defends everyone's rights and freedoms, including making sure everyone has access to high-quality education.

Moreover, she has also advocated for the value of education in impoverished places by using her position as a celebrity. She has advocated for more funding for public education systems and has taken part in several initiatives and events that support education reform.

Natalie Portman has also been a proponent of early childhood education because she understands the critical role it plays in establishing the groundwork for a child's future success. She has backed programs like the Children's Defense Fund's Beat the Odds campaign, which highlights the difficulties high-achieving adolescents from underprivileged homes have in getting a good education while also celebrating their accomplishments.

Lastly, Natalie Portman is committed to promoting and providing financial assistance for education in underserved places, but she goes beyond this. In her efforts, she has also been actively involved, going to different schools and interacting with pupils from all backgrounds. Her advocacy work is informed by her increased understanding of the difficulties these children encounter as a result of these contacts.

In conclusion, Natalie Portman's efforts to promote education in impoverished areas are evidence of her commitment to building a society that is more fair and equal. She has worked tirelessly to promote equal opportunities for all people to access high-quality education through her involvement with organizations like the Genesis Prize Foundation, her support of education reform initiatives, and her practical approach to understanding the challenges faced by students from diverse backgrounds. Others are encouraged to take up advocacy work and help build a brighter future for the next generation through Natalie's efforts.

CHAPTER 5

Iconic Roles and Acting Mastery

Natalie Portman Adapting to Various Characters

Natalie Portman is well known for her ability to change into several personas, which highlights her extraordinary acting skill and commitment to the role. She has portrayed a number of characters that called for her to go through substantial emotional and physical changes during her career, showcasing her adaptability and dedication to making complicated characters come to life on film.

She underwent a significant metamorphosis for her part as Nina in the 2010 psychological thriller "Black Swan," which delves into the world of professional ballet. Natalie worked closely with a ballet instructor and went through a rigorous training program to learn the complex dance moves needed for the part in order to properly inhabit the character. She also made a major weight loss to get the slender, ballet dancer's figure, demonstrating her commitment to the character's metamorphosis.

Also, she showed her commitment to changing for varied characters when she played Jacqueline Kennedy in the film "Jackie" (2016). Natalie studied the previous First Lady's demeanor, speaking habits, and attire in order to perfectly portray her. She further immersed herself in the role by working closely with a dialect coach to develop Kennedy's unique accent.

Natalie Portman's metamorphosis into a young Jewish scientist in the 1998 film "Pi" necessitated her exploration of the field of mathematics and its relationship to spirituality. She studied advanced mathematics and sought advice from subject matter experts to obtain a better knowledge of the material in order to prepare for the position. She was able to play the character with authenticity and depth because of her commitment to study and research.

Furthermore, Natalie Portman plays Alice, a photographer in "Closer" (2004), who is having identity and relationship issues. Natalie researched the nuances of photography to understand the character's line of work and worked closely with a speech coach to develop her British accent in order to fully capture the character's complicated emotional journey.

Her versatility as a character actor extends beyond her cinematic work. She has also shown her flexibility and dedication to her art in her work on stage. She was the lead actress in Mike Nichols' Broadway adaptation of "The Seagull," which opened in 2002. Natalie further cemented her reputation as a talented actor with her portrayal of the disturbed artist Nina, which demonstrated her ability to communicate emotional depth and sensitivity on stage.

In conclusion, Natalie Portman's career has benefited greatly from her transformational acting skills, which have enabled her to play a variety of characters and display her enormous ability. Throughout her career, she has received several awards and received critical praise for her commitment to preparation, study, and character immersion. Natalie's ability to portray sophisticated, nuanced people on stage and in film is shown by her changes in a variety of roles. Her dedication to her profession is evident in her transformations.

Pushing Film and Performance Boundaries

Natalie Portman has continuously pushed limits in both cinema and performance, pushing herself to take on complicated and varied parts that highlight her enormous skill. She has received a lot of praise and recognition for her daring in taking on unusual roles and her commitment to pushing the boundaries of her profession.

Her performance in the 2010 movie "Black Swan" is among the most noteworthy instances of Natalie pushing the envelope in theater and cinema. She played Nina, a ballet dancer who is battling the immense pressure to reach excellence in her art form, in this psychological thriller. For her performance, Natalie had to change drastically both physically and emotionally. She had to learn complex ballet moves and dig deeply into her character's inner struggle. She pushed the bounds of what was expected of her as an actor and cemented her reputation as a dynamic and fearless performer with her devotion to honesty and her craft.

She played former First Lady Jacqueline Kennedy in "Jackie" (2016), a role that required a deep comprehension of the character's personality and historical background. Natalie further submerged herself in Jackie's world by studying Kennedy's demeanor, speaking habits, and attire in order to fully inhabit the role. Her representation of such a historically important character, along with her attention to detail, stretched the bounds of biographical cinema portrayals.

Natalie Portman's readiness to take on difficult and nuanced roles was further shown by her performance in "Closer" (2004). As Alice, a photographer struggling with her identity and relationships, Natalie had to delve into the nuances of her character's psychological development. She studied photojournalism to comprehend the character's line of work and worked closely with a speech coach to develop her British accent in order to prepare for the part. She was able to stretch the limits of her performance and provide an engaging picture of a complex person because of her dedication to preparation and study.

Also, she plays Evey Hammond in the 2005 film "V for Vendetta," a young lady enmeshed in a revolutionary uprising against an oppressive government. In this part, she had to represent a woman who changes from a victim to a strong person in her own right, while still navigating the intricacies of a dystopian future. Natalie excelled in both emotional and action-packed parts, pushing the limits of typical female roles in action movies with her depiction of Evey.

Film and performance frontiers have been pushed in large part because of Natalie's work in indie cinema. She co-starred with Zach Braff as a young lady dealing with mental health problems in the 2004 film "Garden State". In this part, she was able to demonstrate her ability to approach delicate themes with sensitivity and honesty while also delving into the subtleties of mental illness.

Natalie Portman has continuously pushed the envelope in theater and cinema throughout her career, pushing herself to take on demanding and varied parts that highlight her extraordinary skill. In addition to receiving critical praise from all quarters, her willingness to take on challenging roles and her commitment to pushing the boundaries of her profession have encouraged other actors and actresses to reach new heights in their industry. Natalie's dedication to pushing limits in performance and cinema is evidence of her love for what she does and her persistent drive to make work that has an effect and provokes thinking.

Natalie Portman Working Together with Other Actors and Artists

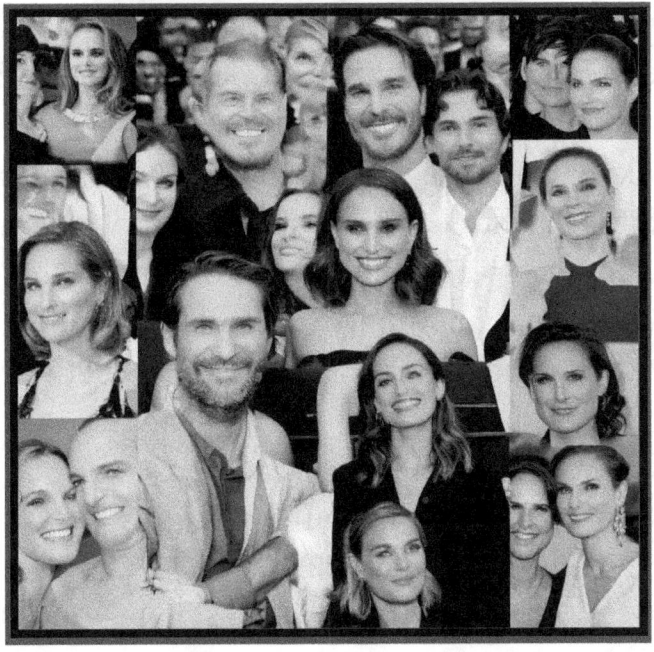

Natalie Portman with actors and actresses

Natalie Portman has often worked with various actors and artists, encouraging one another to provide outstanding performances and building strong creative connections. Along with producing some of the most memorable on-screen moments, these partnerships have helped Natalie develop as an artist and hone her skills.

Working with director Mike Nichols on the Broadway version of "The Seagull" (2002) was one of Natalie's most prominent partnerships. Natalie played Nina in this version of Anton Chekhov's play, a damaged artist who struggles with her identity and relationships. She was able to hone her performing abilities even further by having the opportunity to collaborate directly with an experienced director and benefit from his knowledge.

She appeared on film among an ensemble cast in "Closer" (2004), which also starred Clive Owen, Jude Law, and Julia Roberts. With the help of her co-stars, she was able to delve into the complexity of Alice's character and participate in a dynamic creative process. The film's success may be partly ascribed to the ensemble's excellent performances, which highlight the value of teamwork in the filmmaking process.

Natalie Portman and filmmaker Darren Aronofsky collaborated successfully on "Black Swan" (2010), which received critical praise and several accolades. Natalie portrayed Nina, a ballet dancer who was pushed to the limit of her ability in this psychological thriller. She was able to bring the character's emotional depth to life by directly collaborating with Aronofsky, which produced a stirring and memorable performance.

She returned to her role as Jane Foster from the first "Thor" movie in "Thor: The Dark World" (2013). She worked well with co-stars Anthony Hopkins, Tom Hiddleston, and Chris Hemsworth to give her role a warm, wise quality that enhanced the overall impact of the movie. Through this experience, she was able to showcase her range as an actor by delving into the subtleties of a character inside the framework of a bigger movie world.

Furthermore, cooperation with filmmaker Brady Corbet on the 2018 film "Vox Lux" demonstrates her readiness to collaborate with up-and-coming talent in the field. She played a pop singer dealing with the fallout from a horrific incident in this role. She was able to explore the intricacies of a modern character via this cooperation, showcasing her versatility in a range of roles and genres.

Natalie Portman has continuously pursued partnerships with other actors and artists throughout her career, cultivating deep artistic bonds and encouraging one another to produce extraordinary performances. Along with producing some of the most memorable on-screen moments, these partnerships have helped Natalie develop as an artist and hone her skills. Natalie has shown her dedication to exploring all facets of her acting ability and producing powerful, thought-provoking works by collaborating with a wide variety of talented people.

The Development of Natalie Portman's Acting Style

Over the course of her career, Natalie Portman's acting has changed dramatically, indicating both her development as a creative and her desire to take on challenging parts. From her early days as a child star to her present position as a well-respected and adaptable actor, Natalie has consistently improved her art by experimenting with different acting approaches and embracing new methods.

Her breakthrough performance in "Leon: The Professional" (1994) showcased her innate skill and sensitivity throughout her early career. She had a raw emotional intensity as a young actor that captivated the audience and paved the way for her success in the future. Her early work, however, was mainly distinguished by a more realistic style that let her inherent sensitivity come through.

Natalie Portman's acting evolved to embrace a wider spectrum of emotions and characterizations as her career developed and she experimented with various acting methods and approaches. She demonstrated her ability to play a more nuanced and sophisticated character in "Beautiful Girls" (1996) by using a more nuanced and layered acting technique. This change was a major turning point in her development as an actor and showed that she was capable of playing more mature parts.

She had a dramatic change in her acting technique with "Black Swan" (2010), adopting a more stylized and muscular approach to her role. In order to play the ballet dancer Nina in the movie, she had to undergo a significant physical makeover and learn all of the complicated ballet moves. She gained a greater grasp of the relationship between physicality and emotional expression in acting as a result of this experience, which helped her to build a more dynamic and adaptable acting approach.

Also, has consistently experimented with different acting philosophies and methods across her career, as shown in "Closer" (2004) and "Eve" (2014). She really committed herself to these parts, researching the careers of the characters and honing their accents in order to provide genuine and true-to-life portrayals. Her commitment to preparation and study has helped her hone her acting technique, allowing her to keep her inherent sensitivity and fragility while adding aspects of method acting.

She has adopted a more avant-garde and non-traditional approach to her acting in more recent years. She played former First Lady Jacqueline Kennedy in "Jackie" (2016), which required her to both explore the character's inner anguish and convey the spirit of the historical figure. She researched Kennedy's demeanor, speech patterns, and attire in order to prepare for the part, showcasing her versatility as an actor in adapting her approach to the needs of a certain character and time period.

Natalie Portman's performance in the 2018 film "Annihilation" demonstrated her readiness to accept unusual parts that test her acting abilities. She portrayed a scientist looking into a mystery occurrence in this science fiction thriller, which required her to negotiate the intricacies of a genre movie while still giving a deep and emotionally charged performance. She was able to push the limits of her art and embrace the unknown as she further developed her acting style as a result of this experience.

Lastly, Natalie Portman's acting style has changed throughout the years, which speaks to her development as a creative and her commitment to trying out new methods. Natalie's acting technique has consistently changed over the years, exhibiting her flexibility and dedication to creating powerful, thought-provoking performances. Her early realistic performances have given way to her current acceptance of experimental and atypical parts.

Natalie Portman's Projects in Theater and Dancing

Natalie Portman's career has been greatly aided by her participation in dance and theater, which has given her the opportunity to demonstrate her flexibility and love of the performing arts. She has taken part in several dance and theater shows over her career as an actor, always challenging herself to develop as a performer.

Her portrayal of Anne Frank in the Broadway version of "The Diary of Anne Frank" (1997) was one of her first theatrical experiences. She was able to refine her stage acting abilities via this experience, working with a gifted ensemble cast and receiving direction from director James Lapine. Reviews of the play were favorable, and reviewers praised Natalie's performance for being genuine and having a lot of emotional depth.

When Mike Nichols directed the play "The Seagull," Natalie made a comeback to the Broadway stage in 2002. She played the role of Nina in this rendition of the classic work by Anton Chekhov, a young artist who is having identity and love issues. She was able to hone her performing abilities even further by having the opportunity to collaborate directly with an experienced director and benefit from his knowledge.

Natalie Portman's acting career has benefited greatly from her love of dancing, especially with her Oscar-winning performance in "Black Swan" (2010). Natalie had intense training in ballet methods from previous professional dancers, as well as a significant physical makeover, to prepare for the character of Nina, a ballet dancer pushed to her limits. Her performance in the movie was improved by her devotion to learning the nuances of ballet, which also demonstrated her willingness to take on the difficulties of other artistic mediums.

In 2013, Natalie Portman worked alongside her husband, choreographer Benjamin Millepied, on the dance film "Pina," which was directed by Wim Wenders. A variety of dance routines from the late German choreographer Pina Bausch's repertory were used in the film as a memorial to her. Through her participation in the project, Natalie was able to learn more about contemporary dance and collaborate directly with well-known dancers, which strengthened her affinity for the genre.

With the dance work "Echo Park," which was presented at the New York City Center's Fall for Dance event in 2015, Natalie made her stage debut as a choreographer. The dancers in the work, which was a collaboration with Benjamin Millepied, were from the Los Angeles Dance Project. Through this experience, she was able to present her love of dance in a new way and develop her creative vision as a choreographer.

In addition to advancing her acting profession, Natalie's involvement in dance and theater has given her the opportunity to learn more about a variety of performing arts disciplines. Her commitment to learning a variety of skills and artistic media has made her a well-rounded artist who can produce compelling and unforgettable performances in a range of settings. Natalie Portman has shown her flexibility and dedication to her profession by growing and evolving as an artist by accepting the difficulties of theater and dance.

CHAPTER 6

Social Activism and Humanitarian Work

Natalie Portman Promoting Reproductive Health and Women's Rights

Natalie Portman has been a strong voice for women's rights and reproductive health, utilizing her position to spread the word and encourage change. Her fervent beliefs in reproductive freedom, gender equality, and the value of education for women and girls across the globe serve as the foundation for her work.

She was a founding member of the nonprofit group "Freshwater," which was established in 2004 with the goal of giving poor nations access to clean water and sanitary facilities. Although the organization's primary emphasis is on water-related concerns, it also discusses the connection between women's rights and clean water since women and girls in these areas often shoulder the responsibility of collecting water, which may restrict their access to economic and educational possibilities.

When Natalie joined the Amnesty International campaign as the spokeswoman for Women's Rights in 2005, her dedication to reproductive health and women's rights took a major turn for the better. In this capacity, she strove to increase public awareness of concerns including reproductive rights, gender-based violence, and women's and girls' access to education around the globe.

With her spouse, Benjamin Millepied, Natalie co-founded the "Shma Foundation" in 2006. The charity works to promote educational programs that help Israel's poor children, emphasizing gender equality and female empowerment in particular. Natalie has fought to remove obstacles and provide girls the chance to follow their passions and realize their full potential via the foundation.

Natalie's graduating address at Harvard University in 2015 elevated her campaign for reproductive health and rights to unprecedented heights. During her speech, she demanded more funding for reproductive health care and chastised the institution for lacking on-campus abortion facilities. Her steadfast dedication to guaranteeing women's autonomy over their bodies and access to necessary medical treatment was made clear in her address.

She was elected as the Genesis Prize Foundation's first-ever female president in 2018. The foundation grants yearly prizes to those who have made a substantial contribution to Jewish life and culture. The foundation changed its emphasis under her direction to concentrate on social justice and human rights concerns, such as gender equality and reproductive health. Natalie's commitment to leveraging her power to bring about good change was further shown by her actions.

Natalie Portman has shown a thorough awareness of the connections between women's rights and reproductive health throughout her advocacy efforts. She has established herself as a leading voice in the struggle for reproductive freedom and gender equality by taking up these causes in a variety of positions. Others are encouraged by Natalie's action to become involved in social change and strive for a future where women and girls have equal access to resources and opportunities.

Advocating for Environmental Justifications

Natalie Portman's personal and professional lives are significantly impacted by her dedication to environmental problems. She has continuously promoted sustainable behaviors, helped groups striving for a greener future, and brought attention to environmental challenges using her platform.

She joined the board of trustees of the Natural Resources Defense Council (NRDC), one of the top environmental advocacy organizations in the US, in 2006. The NRDC uses research, activism, and legal action to protect the planet's natural resources and advance a sustainable, healthy environment. Natalie has supported the organization's initiatives to combat climate change, save endangered species, and advance sustainable energy as a board member.

"Freshwater Action," a movement for activism that Natalie started in 2009 in collaboration with the Natural Resources Defense Council. The project sought to address the serious problem of water contamination and its effects on the environment and human health. Natalie advocated for lawmakers to take action on these urgent challenges by working to increase public understanding of the importance of safeguarding freshwater supplies and water conservation via Freshwater Action.

Natalie is an environmental activist who also practices personal responsibility. She has made a strong case for the advantages of veganism and plant-based diets. She joined forces with the nonprofit group "One Meal a Day" in 2019 to promote more sustainable eating practices and a decrease in meat consumption. Natalie has also been a vocal supporter of animal rights, lending her support to groups like PETA and Mercy For

Animals in their campaigns to improve animal welfare and lessen the negative effects of industrial farming on the environment.

Along with her husband, Benjamin Millepied, Natalie co-founded the "Animal Content Index" (ACI) in 2010. Film and television makers may use the ACI database to find and replace animal-based material in their films with plant-based substitutes. The ACI seeks to lessen the demand for animal products and increase public awareness of the effects that human consumption decisions have on the environment and animal welfare by encouraging the adoption of vegan substitutes in the entertainment sector.

Natalie Portman has shown a great dedication to promoting sustainable practices and supporting environmental problems throughout her career. Her participation in a number of organizations and projects has encouraged people to live more environmentally friendly lives and assisted in bringing important environmental concerns to the public's attention. Natalie has emerged as a key player in the battle against climate change and the preservation of our planet's natural resources by using her position to promote a greener future.

Advocating for the Welfare and Rights of Animals

Natalie Portman has been an ardent supporter of animal rights and welfare, utilizing her position to spread the word about the harm that human actions can do to animals and to encourage more humane treatment. Her involvement encompasses a range of animal rights issues, such as the preservation of wildlife, industrial farming, and animal experimentation.

She started supporting People for the Ethical Treatment of Animals (PETA) in 2008; PETA is a group that fights animal abuse and promotes animal rights. Since then, she has taken part in a number of initiatives and activities meant to increase public awareness of the pain that animals endure in a variety of industries, including the fashion, entertainment, and food production sectors.

Her personal life demonstrates her unwavering devotion to animal welfare. Since she was nine years old, she has avoided consuming animal products because she cares about animal welfare and the effects that industrial farming has on the environment. Natalie has advocated for veganism and its advantages for the environment and animals by using her platform to persuade people to follow a plant-based diet.

The documentary "Eating Animals," which was based on Jonathan Safran Foer's book, was narrated by Natalie in 2018. The movie investigates the effects of industrial farming and how our dietary choices affect the environment, human health, and animal welfare. Natalie further demonstrated her commitment to advocating for a more sustainable and humane food system by adding her voice to this effort.

In addition to her involvement with PETA, Natalie has contributed to the causes of animal care and rights. She joined forces with the nonprofit group "One Meal a Day" in 2019 to promote more sustainable eating practices and a decrease in meat consumption. Additionally, she has backed Mercy For Animals, a group that aims to promote plant-based diet alternatives and put a stop to animal abuse in agriculture.

Natalie works in the entertainment sector and is an activist for animal rights and welfare. She and her husband, Benjamin Millepied, co-founded the "Animal Content Index" (ACI) in 2010. Film and television makers may use the ACI database to find and replace animal-based material in their films with plant-based substitutes. The ACI seeks to lessen the demand for animal products and increase public awareness of the effects that human consumption decisions have on the environment and animal welfare by encouraging the adoption of vegan substitutes in the entertainment sector.

Finally, Natalie Portman has emerged as a key player in the struggle for animal rights and welfare as a result of her many projects and alliances. Her commitment to bringing attention to animal suffering and advocating for more humane treatment has motivated people to consider their own actions and make more thoughtful decisions that put the welfare of all living things first.

Natalie Portman Engagement with Social and Political Issues

Natalie Portman has been deeply engaged in political and social concerns, using her position to promote change and increase awareness of numerous causes. Regarding issues like women's rights, reproductive health, education, and the Israeli-Palestinian conflict, she has been very outspoken.

Together with her younger brother Luke, Natalie co-founded "The Beautiful Dream Society" (TBDS) in 2004. By giving them access to education and promoting intercultural understanding, TBDS seeks to enhance the lives of children in Israel and Palestine. Natalie has worked to foster harmony and understanding between the two communities via her organization, highlighting the value of education in building a brighter future for the young people in the area.

She supports women's rights and reproductive health as part of her engagement in political and social concerns. She provided the narration for the 2018 film "On the Basis of Sex," which chronicles the early legal career and advocacy for gender equality of Supreme Court Justice Ruth Bader Ginsburg. Natalie has also supported Planned Parenthood, an institution that helps millions of Americans with their reproductive health needs and sex education.

Also, Natalie Portman garnered media attention in the 2020 US presidential election when she criticized then-President Donald Trump and the practices of his government. She urged her fans on social media to vote for and support politicians who shared her views on matters like women's rights, healthcare, and climate change.
She has been active in political and social concerns in her home country of Israel in addition to her work in the United States.

Regarding the Israeli-Palestinian issue, she has been transparent about her complicated relationship with Israel and her support for a two-state solution. Natalie has urged for a more equitable and peaceful settlement to the continuing conflict and has questioned several of the practices of the Israeli government.

Furthermore, she has always been involved in politics and social concerns; her commitment has never been restricted to any one cause or area. Additionally, she has been a strong advocate for a number of groups and projects that advance social justice, equality, and education. She has, for instance, supported the March for Our Lives campaign, which advocates for changes to gun laws in the US, and taken part in the Time's Up movement, which attempts to end sexual harassment and inequality in the workplace.

Natalie Portman has shown that she is committed to utilizing her position to address political and social concerns via her activism and advocacy. She has gained prominence in the struggle for a more fair and equitable society by bringing attention to these issues and inspiring others to become engaged.

Promoting Civic Engagement and Voter Turnout

Natalie Portman has been a steadfast supporter of promoting civic involvement and voter turnout. Acknowledging the influence of her position, she has made use of a number of venues and occasions to encourage civic engagement and voting, especially among youth and underrepresented groups.

In 2018, Natalie was a co-founder of the nonprofit "Letters of Action," which offers tools and information on how to become engaged to encourage individuals to take up social and political concerns. The group urges its members to become involved in local politics, send letters to their politicians, and take part in community activity.

Natalie Portman aggressively promoted voter turnout and civic duty during the 2020 US presidential election. She disseminated information about voting rights, early voting opportunities, and the significance of participating in municipal and national elections using her social media accounts. Natalie also took part in a number of activities and projects that intended to boost voter participation, especially in communities of color and among youth.

She has also spoken in favor of expanding voting rights and inclusivity. In 2019, she backed the "Voting Rights Advancement Act," a measure designed to provide equal access to voting for all eligible individuals and to prevent voter suppression. In order to boost voter turnout, she has also advocated for the introduction of automated voter registration and more early voting opportunities.

Apart from her endeavors inside the United States, Natalie has also promoted civic duty and voter participation abroad. She took part, for instance, in a campaign in 2015 to encourage voter registration and turnout in Israel, highlighting the significance of civic engagement and active citizenship.

Likewise, she supports a number of groups and programs that promote political action and civic education as part of her efforts to promote voter participation and civic duty. Michelle Obama launched the non-profit group "When We All Vote," which seeks to boost civic engagement and voter turnout in the US. She has been working with the organization. Natalie has further backed the "Youth Vote Coalition," an alliance of institutions committed to fostering youth civic involvement and involving them in the electoral process.

Lastly, she has gained prominence in urging people to take part in the political process via her support of voter participation and civic duty. She has motivated people to actively participate in influencing their communities and the wider globe by highlighting the significance of voting and civic engagement.

CHAPTER 7

Managing her Personal and Professional Lives

Natalie Portman Getting Married and Having Kids

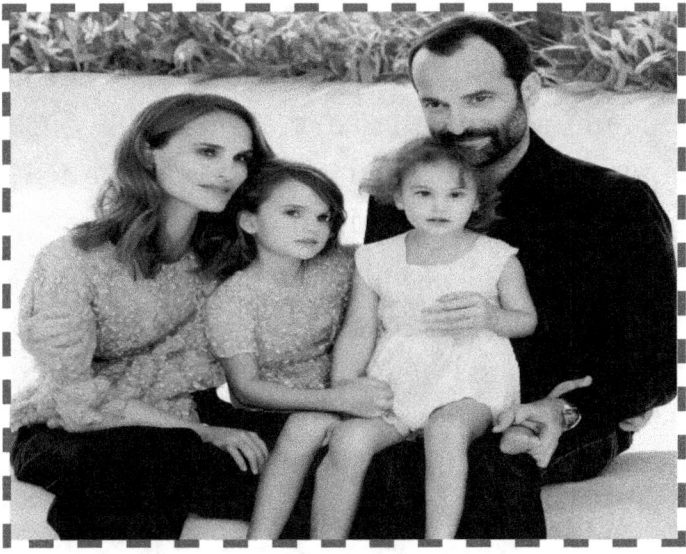

Natalie Portman, Benjamin Millepied, Aleph and Amalia

Natalie Portman's path to motherhood and love has been an amazing and very personal one. Her experiences as an actor, activist, and public person have been greatly influenced by her relationship with her husband, Benjamin Millepied, and their children.

2009's "Black Swan" film set was where Natalie and French dancer and choreographer Benjamin Millepied first connected. After falling in love, they were joined in marriage in 2012 in Big Sur, California, in a modest Jewish ceremony. Because of their shared appreciation of the arts, Benjamin and Natalie have a close relationship. Benjamin choreographed for numerous of Natalie's films, including "Black Swan" and "Song to Song."

Prior to the premiere of "Black Swan," in 2011, Natalie revealed that she was expecting their first child. Aleph, the couple's son, was born in June 2011. Natalie balanced her profession and motherhood by going on to work in the film business while raising her kid.

Amalia, a daughter, was born in 2017 to Natalie and her partner. Natalie's life has changed significantly as a result of being a mother of two, both emotionally and professionally. She has discussed the difficulties and rewards of being a mom, emphasizing the need to strike a balance between career and family life.

Furthermore, Natalie Portman's activism and advocacy activities have been affected by her experiences as a mother. She has fought for women's rights, access to contraception, and education, seeing the significance of these causes through her own mothering experiences. Natalie has also advocated for more resources and assistance for working parents and has been outspoken about the difficulties experienced by working moms in the entertainment sector.

Natalie Portman's connection with Benjamin Millepied and their kids has given her a greater sense of purpose, love, and happiness. She has found support and motivation from their family in her personal life as well as in her career as an activist and actor. Natalie's experience being a mother has changed the way she views the world, love, and the value of a family.

Natalie Portman Balanced Family and Work Together

Natalie Portman has always been a committed actor and activist, being a mother has had a big impact on how she approaches her career and personal life. For Natalie, finding a balance between her professional and parental obligations has been an ongoing learning process, but she has succeeded in both areas.

She encountered the difficulties of juggling her profession with her new duty as a parent when she became a mother for the first time in 2011. She has been candid in discussing the challenges of balancing career and family obligations, especially in the demanding realm of Hollywood. In order to meet her children's needs and pursue a successful acting and advocacy career, Natalie had to negotiate the challenges of being a working mother.

Also, she has made deliberate decisions and set priorities for her time in order to maintain a healthy balance between her family and career. She has made sure that her job is meaningful and enjoyable by carefully choosing initiatives that reflect her values and views. This has made it possible for her to continue being there for her kids while also having a strong sense of purpose and passion for her work.

Natalie has also made a strong case for the importance of providing working parents in the entertainment business with more tools and assistance. She has advocated for more daycare choices, flexible work schedules, and companies that are sensitive to the difficulties experienced by working moms. Natalie hopes to improve the supportive atmosphere for parents in the sector by pushing for these improvements, which will enable them to prioritize their jobs without sacrificing their family time.

However, she has made a deliberate effort to be an engaged and present mom in addition to her professional endeavors. She has spoken about how important it is to spend quality time with her kids and include them in activities that support their development. This entails actively participating in their education, fostering their hobbies, and creating a secure and supportive atmosphere in which they may flourish.

One important component of Natalie Portman's life has been finding a balance between her family and career. Her commitment to her kids and profession has helped her to succeed in all areas, serving as a role model for those juggling the demands of work-life balance. Natalie's strategy for striking a balance between her personal and professional lives shows how dedicated she is to her roles as a mother, accomplished actor, and activist.

Natalie Portman Placing Value on her Well-Being and Self-Care

Natalie Portman places a high value on her well-being and self-care because they allow her to preserve her physical and mental health and set an example for others. Natalie is an accomplished actress, activist, and mother who knows how to balance the demands of her hectic schedule by placing a high priority on self-care.

She has discussed the significance of maintaining a healthy lifestyle, which includes consistent exercise, a diet that is balanced, and enough sleep. She has mentioned how much she enjoys dancing and yoga, which help her remain mentally and emotionally well in addition to keeping her physically active. Natalie's self-care regimen has included yoga in particular as it helps her reduce stress, increase her flexibility, and preserve her general well-being.

Moreover, she emphasizes the importance of mental and emotional well-being in addition to physical self-care. She has discussed the value of going to therapy and keeping up a support network in order to deal with life's obstacles. Natalie has been transparent about her battles with depression and anxiety, highlighting the transformative potential that comes from talking about mental health concerns and getting competent assistance.

Furthermore, Natalie's devotion to social and environmental problems is a reflection of her commitment to self-care. As an activist, she has brought attention to animal rights, education, and climate change using her platform. Natalie shows that self-care is about more than just one's own well-being; it's also about serving the larger good by giving these concerns top priority.

In addition to assisting her in maintaining a healthy lifestyle, Natalie's attitude to self-care and wellbeing has improved her as an activist, actor, and mother. She can efficiently handle her tasks and carry on having a beneficial influence on the world if she puts her own health first.

To sum up, Natalie Portman's commitment to well-being and self-care is a fundamental aspect of who she is. She provides an example for others to follow by putting her physical, mental, and emotional well-being first and leading a more balanced and satisfying life. In addition to helping her personally, Natalie's dedication to self-care advances both the environment and society.

Handling Priorities and Time Management

Natalie Portman's ability to effectively manage her time and prioritize her responsibilities is essential to her success in her positions as an activist, actor, and mother. A deliberate approach to time management and priority planning is necessary to juggle a busy profession with a family, personal hobbies, and other commitments.

She has been candid about the difficulties she has balancing her personal and professional lives, especially in the hectic realm of Hollywood. She has created a regimented schedule that helps her efficiently manage her time and concentrate on her most important duties. This involves establishing specific goals and targets for her personal and professional lives, since doing so keeps her motivated and organized.

Setting her family as her first priority is one of Natalie's main time management techniques. She knows how important it is to be there for her kids and to make time for their needs since she is a mother. To ensure that her employment does not conflict with her duty as a parent, she must carefully choose initiatives that reflect her values and views.

She puts her health and well-being above everything else, even her family. She understands the value of maintaining a healthy lifestyle that consists of consistent exercise, a well-balanced diet, and enough sleep. Natalie can better manage her workload and have a happy attitude in life if she puts her own health first.

Also, her dedication to a number of social and environmental problems also influences how she manages her time and sets priorities. As an activist, she has brought attention to animal rights, education, and climate change using her platform. Natalie shows that she appreciates her role in having a good influence on society and the environment by volunteering her time for these causes.

Natalie has been able to succeed in her many positions while keeping a feeling of balance and satisfaction because of her approach to time management and priority setting. Through prioritizing her family, self-care, and advocacy, she has crafted a fulfilling and meaningful life that is not simply prosperous. Others who are struggling to strike a balance between job, family, and personal interests might draw inspiration from Natalie's time management abilities and prioritizing techniques.

Natalie Portman Helping Out Other Working Parents

Natalie Portman has been a strong supporter of working parents, acknowledging the particular difficulties they have in juggling work and family obligations. Given her own experience as a mother, she recognizes the value of fostering an atmosphere at work where parents feel supported and encouraged to thrive in both their personal and professional lives.

She is primarily concerned with understanding workplaces and advocating for flexible work options. Offering working parents flexible work hours and remote work possibilities, in her opinion, may greatly help them manage their time and obligations. This enhances work-life balance and aids in the retention of brilliant people who would find it difficult to manage their obligations to their families and jobs in the absence of this.

Natalie has also pushed for accessible and reasonably priced daycare options. She feels that offering working parents high-quality childcare alternatives is crucial to their overall professional success and well-being. Natalie hopes to make it simpler for working parents to achieve their career ambitions without sacrificing their family life by supporting laws and programs that enhance the daycare infrastructure.

In addition, she also stresses how crucial it is to have a welcoming workplace that recognizes and honors the contributions made by working parents. This entails providing tools and chances for career advancement in addition to cultivating an environment that values candid dialogue and comprehension. Natalie feels that working parents may succeed both emotionally and professionally by encouraging a supportive work environment.

Natalie's dedication to helping other working parents goes beyond her own convictions. She has advocated for legislative reforms that may have an impact and raised awareness of the difficulties encountered by working parents by using her position as a celebrity and activist. By doing this, she has encouraged others to follow in her footsteps and build a more welcoming and encouraging atmosphere for working parents.

In conclusion, Natalie Portman's commitment to helping other working parents demonstrates her empathy and comprehension of the particular difficulties experienced by anyone trying to combine work and family obligations. Natalie is fighting to create a world where working parents can succeed both emotionally and professionally by promoting flexible work schedules, reasonably priced daycare, and encouraging work environments.

CHAPTER 8

The Influence of Natalie Portman in the 21st Century

Motivating Upcoming Actors and Activist of the Next Generations

Beyond her activism and acting career, Natalie Portman has a lasting impact because she is an inspiration to the next generations of activists and performers. Her devotion to social problems and her passion for her profession have produced a model that others might follow and strive for.

Natalie is a role model for budding actresses in part because of her ability to manage her personal and professional lives. Natalie serves as an example of how it is possible to succeed in the entertainment business and yet feel fulfilled by prioritizing her family and using time management skills. For young performers who may find it difficult to adjust to the demands of the business and understand the value of establishing limits, this is a priceless lesson.

For the next generations of performers and activists, Natalie's dedication to action serves as an inspiration. Her commitment to a range of environmental and social concerns, including animal rights, education, and climate change, demonstrates the effectiveness of leveraging one's platform to effect good change. Natalie is now seen as an inspiration to others who want to change the world because of the way she has combined her activism and acting profession.

Natalie has continuously pushed herself to take on varied and difficult parts throughout her career, inspiring the next generations of performers. This includes the part she played as a dancer battling the demands of her career in "Black Swan," for which she won an Oscar. Through accepting challenging and thought-provoking parts, Natalie inspires young actors to push the limits of their craft and not be afraid to take on challenging material.

Her methodical and enthusiastic approach to lobbying serves as an example for upcoming activists. She has engaged in direct action and policy reforms in addition to using her platform to bring attention to a number of causes. For those who want to have a significant influence both within and outside of their communities, this blend of activism and advocacy offers important lessons.

In addition, Natalie's commitment to mentoring and teaching has greatly influenced the next generation of performers and campaigners. She has participated in a number of educational projects, such as visiting Harvard University as a lecturer. Through imparting her wisdom and life experiences, Natalie encourages others to follow their dreams and change the world.

In summary, Natalie Portman will have a significant influence on the next acting and activism generations. For those hoping to follow in her footsteps, her capacity to manage her professional and personal lives, her devotion to social issues, her readiness to take on difficult responsibilities, and her commitment to mentoring and education are all important lessons. Natalie's impact will persist in motivating and molding the next cohort of artists and campaigners.

Considering Her Legacy and the Future of Her Career Development

It is important to consider Natalie Portman's legacy and the future as her career develops. Her path has been characterized by a blend of personal development, social engagement, and creative accomplishments, all of which have added to her lasting influence on the entertainment business and beyond.

Natalie's impact is mostly shaped by her dedication to pushing the envelope in her acting profession. She has constantly selected parts that push her as an artist and give her the freedom to explore a variety of personalities and emotions over her career in the business. Her willingness to take chances has not only brought her praise from critics but also encouraged other performers to embark on challenging roles.

Her legacy has also been significantly shaped by her advocacy. She has shown the value of leveraging one's position to advocate for several social and environmental problems. Her commitment to changing the world has motivated a great number of people to take up activism and raise awareness of the problems that our planet faces.

Additionally, her emphasis on mentoring and education will probably continue to shape her legacy as she looks to the future. She has inspired many people to follow their interests and change the world by imparting her expertise and experiences to newer generations. Her dedication to fostering talent will surely help the next generation of artists and activists to continue her work.

Therefore, she sets a great example for people in the entertainment business by managing her personal and professional lives in addition to her creative and activism endeavors. She has shown that it is possible to attain success while retaining a feeling of contentment and well-being by prioritizing her family and establishing limits. Those navigating the difficulties of the entertainment industry will continue to find resonance in this facet of her legacy.

In the future, Natalie Portman's development as an artist, activist, and mentor will surely influence her legacy. Her influence on the world will only increase as she develops more and finds new ways to express herself. Future generations will continue to be inspired and influenced by her commitment to utilizing her platform for good change, her willingness to take on difficult jobs, and her devotion to developing the potential of the next generation.

In conclusion, Natalie Portman's legacy bears witness to her many accomplishments in both the entertainment sector and society at large. Her emphasis on creative development, social activity, personal balance, and mentoring will continue to define her influence for years to come as she considers her path and looks to the future.

Natalie Portman; A Classic Icon for All Time

Natalie Portman's long influence and numerous abilities are shown by her ageless appeal and legendary stature in the entertainment business. She has inspired future generations and gone above and beyond the call of duty as a renowned actress, mentor, and activist.

She has shown an unrelenting dedication to her craft throughout her career, always selecting parts that push her artistic boundaries and give her the freedom to explore a broad spectrum of emotions and personalities. Her commitment to development and betterment has not only brought her praise from critics but also cemented her place in history as an iconic figure.

Her continuing popularity has also been greatly influenced by her activism and generosity. She has shown that the potential of leveraging one's platform for good change can have a lasting effect on the globe by supporting a variety of social and environmental concerns. She has gained the respect of many people and solidified her place in history as an icon thanks to her unwavering efforts to build a brighter future.

As a teacher and mentor, Natalie has inspired the next generation to follow their interests and change the world by imparting her wisdom and experiences. Her legendary position has been further cemented by her dedication to developing talent and encouraging progress, as she continues to motivate and impact upcoming artists and activists.

Natalie's ageless attractiveness is also attributed to her ability to maintain a healthy work-life balance. She has shown that it is possible to attain success while retaining a feeling of contentment and well-being by prioritizing her family and establishing limits. She has gained friends and admirers because of her relatable nature, which has elevated her to the status of a timeless legend.

In the future, as Natalie Portman develops and finds new ways to express herself, her ageless appeal will only increase. Her reputation as an icon will be perpetuated for years to come because of her devotion to utilizing her platform for good, her willingness to take on difficult assignments, and her nurturing of the next generation of talent.

In summary, Natalie Portman's enduring popularity stems from her diverse contributions to both the entertainment business and society at large. She has inspired future generations and gone above and beyond the call of duty as an actress, activist, mentor, and role model. People of all ages will continue to be moved by her lasting influence and legendary reputation, making her a real timeless figure.

Natalie Portman's Impact on Girls and Young Women

A major part of Natalie Portman's legacy is her impact on young women and girls. She has been an inspiration and role model to innumerable people who want to change the world. Through her many pursuits, she has inspired others to follow their dreams and interests and shown the value of utilizing one's platform for good.

She has had a significant effect on young women and girls via her advocacy, among other things. She has shown how the strength of standing out for what one believes in may lead to a brighter future for everyone by supporting social and environmental concerns. Many young women and girls have been encouraged to become involved in activism and raise their awareness of the problems that our planet faces through this dedication to changing things.

Also, her impact on young women and girls has also been greatly influenced by her commitment to mentoring and education. She has inspired many others to follow their interests and change the world by imparting her expertise and experiences. In addition to inspiring future artists, this dedication to developing talent and encouraging development has encouraged young women and girls to become change agents in their communities and beyond.

Furthermore, she has defied gender norms and broken down boundaries as a prominent actor in the entertainment business. Young women and girls have learned from her varied and thought-provoking roles that they can succeed in whatever career they choose, regardless of what society expects of them. Many have been inspired to follow their aspirations and overcome limiting beliefs by this example of tenacity and resolve.

Another way that Natalie influences young women and girls is via her ability to strike a balance between her personal and professional lives. She has shown that it is possible to attain success while retaining a feeling of contentment and well-being by prioritizing her family and establishing limits. Many young women and girls have found resonance in this relevant aspect since they often have comparable difficulties in balancing their personal and professional lives.

In the future, Natalie Portman's impact on young girls and women will only increase as she persists in pushing boundaries and igniting change. Her influence on young women and girls will endure for years to come because of her willingness to take on difficult positions, her commitment to utilizing her platform for good change, and her devotion to developing the next generation of talent.

In conclusion, Natalie Portman's impact on young girls and women is evidence of her many contributions to society. She has inspired numerous others to follow their interests and change the world through her advocacy, mentoring, and personal example. Her impact on young women and girls will only increase as she develops and finds new ways to express herself, guaranteeing that her legacy will motivate the next generations.

The Influence of Public Figures' Genuineness and Empathy

Natalie Portman is a strong role model for those in the entertainment business and beyond because of her honesty and empathy, which have been key factors in her success as a public figure. Her capacity to emotionally connect with people has struck a chord with followers and admirers, underscoring the significance of empathy and genuineness in the realm of public personalities.

Her desire to be honest and sensitive about her experiences, both personal and professional, is a crucial component of her genuineness. She has gained the affection of her followers by being relatable and sharing her triumphs and setbacks. She has also been able to establish a stronger connection with her audience via her genuine approach, going beyond the usual celebrity-fan dynamic.

She displays a real interest in other people's well-being, which shows that her empathy goes beyond her own existence. Her altruism and activism stem from a profound awareness of the struggles that many areas and people endure. She has been able to effect significant change and encourage others to follow suit thanks to her sympathetic attitude.

Public personalities like Natalie Portman demonstrate the importance of sincerity and empathy in their capacity to engage their audience on a deeper level. This relationship develops admiration, trust, and respect, all of which have the potential to have a greater influence on society. Public personalities like Natalie have the power to inspire good change and build a more compassionate society by being true to themselves and really caring about others. Apart from her personal attributes, Natalie's genuineness and compassion have also impacted her decisions in her professional life. She has continuously looked for jobs that let her explore nuanced emotions and people, showcasing her profound comprehension of the human condition. Her reputation as a potent role model for other public people and aspiring artists has been further cemented by her dedication to honesty in her work.

Natalie Portman's dedication to genuineness and empathy will surely always be a guiding concept in her life and work as she develops and grows. Her inspiring example serves as a poignant reminder of the value of being loyal to oneself and showing compassion in the always-shifting entertainment scene and beyond.

To sum up, Natalie Portman's genuineness and empathy, which have enabled her to engage her audience more deeply and spur constructive change, are the keys to her success as a public figure. In addition to being a major factor in her long-term success, her commitment to being true to herself and showing real concern for others has served as a model for other public figures and aspiring artists. Natalie will surely continue to have an impact on future generations as she leaves her imprint on the globe.

CHAPTER 9

Crafting Effective Narratives

Natalie Portman Developing Scripts and Screenwriting

Natalie Portman's engagement in screenplay creation and scripting demonstrates her versatility and dedication to the craft of storytelling. She has shown to have a thorough knowledge of the craft and the significance of well-developed screenplays in creating captivating storylines by actively participating in the production of her own projects.

With her 2006 film "Everybody Says I Love You," which she co-wrote the screenplay for with renowned filmmaker Woody Allen, Natalie made her screenwriting debut. Her future writing aspirations were paved with this experience, and she further refined her craft by working with other accomplished screenwriters.

She has made a significant contribution to screenwriting with her picture "Black Swan" in 2010. Natalie was extensively engaged in the script's creation, collaborating with director Darren Aronofsky and screenwriter Andres Heinz, in addition to playing the major role of Nina. Because of their partnership, a compelling and very emotional drama was produced, and Natalie was awarded the Academy Award for Best Actress.

However, she is not only involved in her own work but also helps with screenplay creation. She has also spoken in favor of encouraging up-and-coming screenwriters. Together with her husband, Benjamin Millepied, she co-founded the production business Handsomecharlie Films in 2015. The company's goal is to create excellent content that highlights a range of voices and viewpoints, with an emphasis on developing up-and-coming talent in the field.
Natalie Portman has shown via her efforts in screenwriting and screenplay development how important a well-written script is to telling

gripping tales. Her commitment to the craft of storytelling has benefited her own career and encouraged others to follow their love for screenwriting and filmmaking.

Also, her colleagues and the industry at large have acknowledged her dedication to the discipline of screenwriting and screenplay development. Her successes in this field are evidence of her adaptability and commitment to the filmmaking craft. Natalie will surely continue to have a big impact on the screenwriting and screenplay development industries as she develops as an artist and storyteller.

Finally, one of the most important facets of Natalie Portman's diverse career has been her engagement in screenwriting and screenplay creation. Her commitment to the trade has improved her own works and encouraged others to follow their love for narrative. Natalie's influence on the screenplay and script development community will only increase as she works with more accomplished authors and filmmakers, cementing her reputation as a pioneer in the entertainment business.

Natalie Portman Character Development Process in Acting

Natalie Portman's remarkable acting abilities and her commitment to the art of performance are shown by her ability to make characters come to life on film. Her distinct method of character building includes a thorough comprehension of the motives, feelings, and past of the character, enabling her to produce complex, multifaceted depictions that enthrall viewers.

She does a lot of research, which is one of the main components of her character-building process. She explores the character's upbringing, past, and experiences in order to fully comprehend their behaviors and views. Reading books, articles, and screenplays as well as speaking with specialists in a range of subjects pertaining to the character's life are common methods of research.

Natalie Portman uses her own experiences and feelings in addition to research to help her relate to the characters she plays. She is able to give her performances an authenticity that connects with audiences by referencing her personal experiences and emotions. Her method relies heavily on her ability to draw from her own feelings and experiences in order to create authentic, accessible characters that viewers can emotionally identify with.

Cooperation with directors, co-stars, and other members of the production crew is a crucial part of Natalie's character development process. Her comprehension of the character and their role in the plot is improved by the advice and insights she receives from her other artists, which she cherishes. She is able to develop a deep, shared picture of the character because of this collaborative approach, which eventually raises the standard of the movie as a whole.

Furthermore, she puts a lot of effort into preparing for every part, which shows how committed she is to making characters come to life. In order to really inhabit the role she is playing, she often goes through physical changes, language instruction, and other forms of training. Her love for acting and her drive to provide the most genuine and captivating performances possible are evident in her dedication to the trade.

Natalie Portman has shown her extraordinary ability as an actor by bringing a wide variety of roles to life on film throughout her career. Natalie has continuously shown that she is capable of giving life to intricate, multifaceted characters, as seen by her Oscar-winning performance in "Black Swan" and her legendary depiction of Padmé Amidala in the "Star Wars" prequels.

To sum up, Natalie Portman uses a collaborative approach to acting, a great deal of study, and her own experiences to help her bring characters to life on film. Fans and journalists alike have praised her greatly for her commitment to the profession and her ability to develop real, approachable characters. Natalie's influence on the performing arts and cinema industries will surely never diminish as she develops as an artist, serving as an inspiration to upcoming performers and directors.

Working Together with Directors and Screenwriters

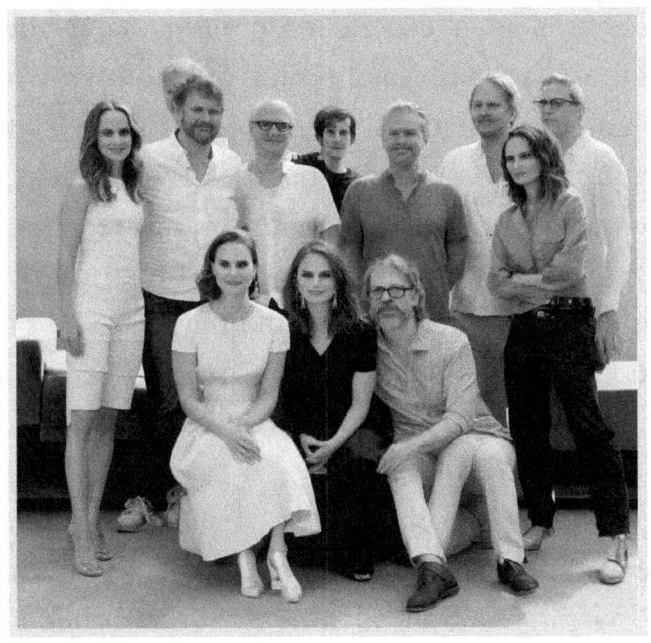

Natalie Portman and Directors and Screenwriters

Natalie Portman's acting career and the success of the projects she has been involved in have been greatly influenced by her partnerships with directors and screenwriters. Her performances have become richer and more complex as a result of these collaborations, which have enabled her to go deeper into the roles she plays. Establishing transparent and honest communication lines with her creative colleagues is a crucial component of Natalie's collaborative approach. She promotes an open exchange of ideas and viewpoints, which eventually strengthens the creative process, by cultivating an atmosphere of mutual respect and trust. She may improve her interpretation of the character and their role in the narrative by being receptive to criticism and ideas from others, which leads to more engaging and genuine performances.

She often collaborates extensively with screenwriters to build the character and improve the narrative. She is able to comprehend the character and their behaviors more fully by talking with the writer about the character's motives, past, and emotional journeys. By working together, the scriptwriter is able to give the character a more complex and realistic representation while simultaneously making sure that Natalie's own take on the part is faithfully captured on film.

Also, she brings her own thoughts and viewpoints to the table while working with filmmakers, but she also cherishes their vision and creative direction. She is aware that the director is in charge of overseeing the project's overall creative vision and making sure that every component functions as a whole. Natalie helps create a common vision that is advantageous to the whole production by acknowledging the director's vision and adding her own perspectives.

When interacting with other members of the production crew, including producers, costume designers, and cinematographers, Natalie adopts a collaborative approach. She is open to hearing everyone's opinions and recommendations since she understands how important each person's participation is to the finished result. Her willingness to work with others makes it possible for her to get a deeper comprehension of the objectives and difficulties of the project, which in turn influences her performance and enables her to develop a more comprehensive portrait of the character.

Natalie Portman has had the privilege of collaborating with some of the most accomplished filmmakers and screenwriters in the business during her career. Her growth as an artist has also been facilitated by these partnerships, in addition to her success as an actor. She has been able to bring a wide variety of characters to life on screen, engaging viewers and making a lasting impression on the film and performing industries by cultivating strong, fruitful connections with her creative collaborators.

Natalie Portman's Engagement with Short Films and Documentaries

In addition to her roles in feature films, Natalie Portman has acted in a number of documentaries and short films, demonstrating her flexibility and dedication to conveying gripping tales. Her body of work has been further enhanced by these pursuits, which have enabled her to experiment with many subjects, genres, and narrative styles.

Natalie Portman created, directed, and performed in the 2004 short film "Eve," which was one of her first attempts at documenting a story. Her filmmaking ability was on display as the picture, which tackles themes of love, sorrow, and the human condition was praised by critics. This experience proved her versatility as a multi-role performer behind the camera and cemented her interest in documentaries and short films.

She has continued to work on documentaries with various directors throughout her career. One such partnership was in the 2013 documentary "The Pyramid," which highlighted the life of the indigenous Chiricahua people of Mexico, directed by the well-known Luc Jacquet. Through her participation in this project, Natalie was able to learn more about the community's history and culture while emphasizing the value of protecting their distinctive legacy.

Also, she has participated in a number of short films in addition to her work in documentaries, often acting as an actor, writer, or producer. Her ability to explore many personalities and themes that would not be possible within the confines of a major picture has been made possible by these ventures. Natalie demonstrated her ability to address difficult emotional subjects when she played a woman coping with the fallout from a broken romance in the 2006 short film "Hotel Chevalier," which was directed by Wes Anderson.

Furthermore, she has supported other filmmakers and their work in addition to her participation in documentaries and short films. She has worked as an executive producer on a number of films, including the social and environmental documentaries "Eating Animals" (2017) and "The Seer and the Unseen" (2019). Natalie has further shown her dedication to leveraging her platform for good change by bringing significant stories to light by lending her resources and influence to these initiatives.

Lastly, she has shown her commitment to storytelling in a variety of media via her involvement in documentaries and short films. Her involvement in these initiatives has given her the chance to work with many artists, investigate novel ideas, and support the larger cinema industry. Through persistently broadening her perspectives and welcoming a variety of artistic chances, Natalie has cemented her reputation as a gifted and adaptable actor and director.

The Storytelling Landscape in the Digital Age

For artists like Natalie Portman, the future of narrative in the digital era offers both a wealth of potential and problems as technology develops further. The use of cutting-edge technology like artificial intelligence, virtual reality, and immersive storytelling platforms has the power to completely change how we interact with and consume tales.

Natalie Portman has shown that she is interested in investigating the opportunities presented by these emerging technologies. Natalie Portman is a fervent advocate for creative storytelling methods. She thinks that a greater variety of views may be heard because of the digital era's ability to provide a platform for more inclusive and varied storytelling. She sees a future where storytelling becomes even more approachable, captivating, and powerful by embracing these developments.

She has shown interest in a number of digital storytelling trends, including the use of virtual reality (VR) technology. Virtual reality (VR) enables users to interact with the environment and completely immerse themselves in a narrative, allowing them to experience it from numerous angles. Natalie has voiced her enthusiasm about how virtual reality (VR) might provide narrative experiences that are more profoundly emotional and transformational.

The use of artificial intelligence (AI) in storytelling is another fascinating feature of the digital era, according to Natalie. With the use of AI, stories may become more flexible and customized, letting audiences interact with the content in a manner that suits their unique tastes and experiences. With the help of this technology, tales might be consumed in a whole new form that is both personalized and interesting for each viewer.

In addition to these innovative tools, Natalie understands the value of using social media sites to share stories. Social media, which has billions of users worldwide, offers artists a never-before-seen chance to share their work, engage with their audience, and create a feeling of community around their narratives. Natalie has been a frequent user of social media, sharing her artistic experiences and advocating for issues close to her heart.

As the narrative landscape in the digital era develops, Natalie Portman is dedicated to discovering new opportunities for artistic expression. She recognizes that there are drawbacks to using technology in storytelling, including the possibility of over-reliance on it or tale standardization. She does, however, think that storytellers may use technology to produce even more powerful and meaningful tales for audiences worldwide if they embrace these developments and keep their attention on the human experience.

Ultimately, Natalie Portman's engagement with the evolution of narrative in the digital era is indicative of her unwavering dedication to being at the forefront of artistic innovation. In the always-changing world of digital storytelling, she hopes to make tales that are more effective, inclusive, and engaging for audiences by embracing new platforms and technology.

CHAPTER 10

Honors, Commendations, and Appreciation

Natalie Portman's Nominations and Oscar Winnings

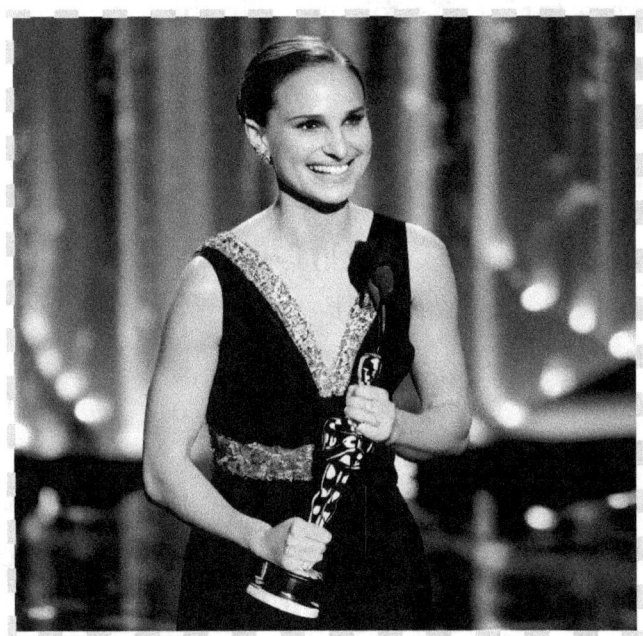

The actress Natalie Portman is well-known and has received a lot of attention during her career for her outstanding work. She has been nominated for and won many Oscars for her roles. These esteemed honors are proof of her brilliance, commitment, and capacity to capture nuanced, multifaceted personalities on film.

A significant professional achievement for Natalie Portman came in 2011 when she was named the Academy Award winner for Best Actress for her performance in the movie "Black Swan." This psychological thriller, which was directed by Darren Aronofsky, centers on the lives of ballet dancer Nina Sayers, played by Natalie Portman, as she battles the demands of her line of work and her fierce rivalry with Mila Kunis's character, Lily. Numerous reviewers hailed Portman's performance in "Black Swan" as one of her greatest ever, and it received widespread accolades.

Natalie Portman was nominated for an Academy Award in the Best Supporting Actress category before she won the Oscar for her performance in the 2004 picture "Closer." Jude Law, Clive Owen, Julia Roberts, and Natalie Portman are among the ensemble cast members of this Mike Nichols-directed drama that Portman leads in. In the movie, Portman's character Alice navigates a complicated web of connections and emotions as it examines the complexity of love and relationships. She deservedly received the nomination for her depiction of a young lady navigating the contemporary world while looking for identity and love.

She has been recognized for her acting abilities with many additional honors and nominations, in addition to her Oscar wins and nominations. She has received recognition for her exceptional work in a number of movies, including a Screen Actors Guild Award, a BAFTA Award, and a Golden Globe Award. Her reputation as a gifted and adaptable actor in the business is further cemented by these honors.

Lastly, she has shown an unshakable dedication to her profession throughout her career, always selecting parts that push her artistic boundaries and give her the chance to delve deeply into human emotion and experience. Her commitment to her career and her talent for captivating audiences with her performances are shown by her Oscar nominations and triumphs. Natalie Portman will undoubtedly continue to get praise and recognition for her extraordinary skill as she develops as an actor.

Natalie Portman Golden Globes and Additional Awards

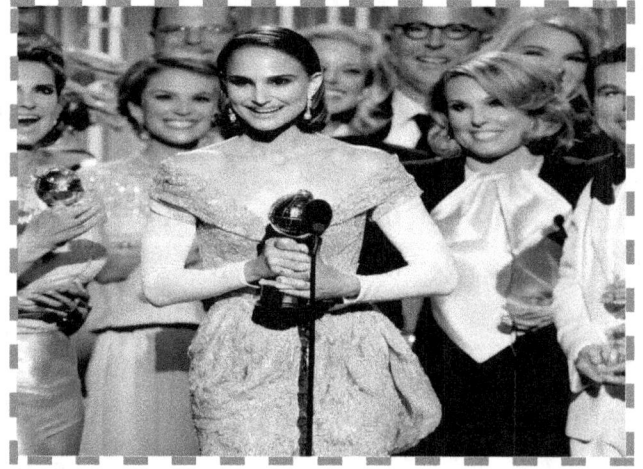

Natalie Portman while receiving Golden Globe Awards

The versatile actress Natalie Portman has received a great deal of praise during her career for her outstanding roles in a number of motion pictures. Apart from her Oscar victories and nominations, she has also received recognition for her skill and commitment to her profession from other esteemed awards shows including the Golden Globes.

The Hollywood Foreign Press Association presents the Golden Globe Awards every year to honor exceptional accomplishments in television and cinema. It is a great honor for Natalie Portman to be given this esteemed award in recognition of her outstanding contributions to the film industry. She won the 2011 Golden Globe for Best Actress in a Dramatic Motion Picture for her outstanding work in "Black Swan." She was able to portray the complexity of a ballet dancer juggling enormous pressure and competition in this performance, which cemented her reputation as one of Hollywood's top actresses.

Throughout her career, Natalie Portman has received other honors in addition to the Golden Globes. She won a 2005 BAFTA Award for Best Actress in a Supporting Role for her work as

Samantha in the movie "Closer." The British Academy of Cinema and Television Arts bestows this award to honor achievement in the media fields of video games, cinema, and television.

Natalie Portman has also received recognition for her skills from the Screen Actors Guild Awards, another important award in the acting community. She was honored with the 2011 SAG Award for Best Performance by a Female Actor in a Leading Role for her work in "Black Swan." The best performances in movies and television, as determined by other actors, are honored with Screen Actors Guild Awards.

Throughout her career, Natalie Portman has received several more distinctions in addition to these noteworthy ones. For her portrayal in "Garden State" (2004), she won the Independent Spirit Award for Best Female Lead. She also won the National Board of Review Award for Best Supporting Actress for her work in "Black Swan." She has also received recognition from the Los Angeles Film Critics Association, the

Satellite Awards, and the Critics' Choice Movie Awards, among other organizations.

Natalie Portman has continuously selected interesting and demanding parts that let her delve into the subtleties of human emotions and experiences. Her many accolades and distinctions attest to her dedication to her work and her capacity to enthrall audiences with her performances. Natalie Portman will definitely continue to be acknowledged for her extraordinary skill and commitment to her career as an actor.

The Effect of Her Career's Critical Acclaim

The praise Natalie Portman has gotten from critics over her acting career has had a big influence on her profession. Her professional status has increased as a result of this recognition, which has also made a wide variety of responsibilities and possibilities more accessible to her. The favorable reactions to her work have been important in molding her professional path and establishing her as one of the industry's most esteemed and renowned actresses.

Alongside Susan Sarandon, Portman acted in the 1999 film "Anywhere But Here," which marked one of the biggest turning points in her career. The film, which was directed by Wayne Wang, tells the tale of a mother and daughter team. Portman's character, Adele, wants to succeed in Hollywood and leave their little village behind. Although there were differing opinions on the movie, Portman's performance was highly appreciated, gaining her recognition from both critics and viewers and securing her a Golden Globe nomination. Her early success prepared the path for her to pursue more difficult parts in the future and for her to keep developing as an actor.

As her career developed, Portman's performances in a number of movies won her praise from critics. Her performance in the drama "Garden State," directed by Zach Braff in 2005, earned praise and strengthened her reputation as a gifted performer. Her depiction of a young lady dealing with mental health problems was well-received by both reviewers and viewers, leading to her being nominated for a Broadcast Film Critics Association Award.

The praise Portman earned from critics for her roles in "Closer" (2004) and "V for Vendetta" (2006) strengthened her reputation as a talented and adaptable actor. She portrayed a young lady skillfully navigating the complexity of love and relationships in "Closer," and in "V for Vendetta," she played Evey Hammond, a teenager caught up in a political rebellion. Her ability to portray a variety of personalities and take on difficult issues was seen in these performances, which won her praise from both audiences and critics.

Significant movie office success has also resulted from Natalie Portman's critical praise. In addition to bringing her financial success, her parts in popular movies like the "Star Wars" prequels and the "Thor" trilogy in the Marvel Cinematic Universe have given her the chance to demonstrate her acting versatility in high-profile productions. Portman's flexibility as an actor and her ongoing attraction to both critics and audiences are shown by her ability to strike a balance between critical praise and commercial success.

In conclusion, Natalie Portman's career has been greatly impacted by critical praise. Her reputation as a recognized actor has grown as a result of the praise she has earned for her performances, which has also helped her get a number of parts and strike a balance between critical and financial success. Portman's commitment to her art and the favorable reactions to her creations will surely continue to influence her prosperous and significant profession as she develops as an artist.

The Value of Acknowledgment in the Entertainment Sector

In the very competitive and dynamic entertainment sector, actors, directors, writers, and other professionals rely heavily on recognition to shape their careers. Acknowledgement in the form of honors, prizes, and critical acclaim is valuable to a person such as Natalie Portman, who has had a huge effect on the film industry. It may validate her skills, elevate her professional status, and lead to new chances.

First and foremost, acknowledgement confirms the skill, effort, and commitment of an artist such as Natalie Portman. An actor's extraordinary talent and dedication to their art are shown when their performance is recognized with renowned accolades like the Oscars, Golden Globes, or BAFTAs. This affirmation strengthens their sense of self-worth and solidifies their standing as an esteemed and well-liked personality in the field.

Second, being well-known may greatly raise an artist's profile in the public eye as well as inside their business. A star like Natalie Portman gains notoriety and becomes more in demand by producers, directors, and other business people when they get continuous recognition for their performances. Their future projects may see more creative freedom, bigger parts, and more lucrative offers as a result of the growing demand for their expertise.

In the entertainment sector, recognition may also lead to new possibilities and collaborative efforts. When an actor receives recognition for their performance, other skilled professionals could reach out to them, wanting to work with them on exciting new projects. Without the initial attention and following possibilities, these partnerships would not have resulted in the development of pioneering and significant works.

In Natalie Portman's instance, the praise she has earned from critics has shown her abilities and given her access to a wide variety of jobs and chances. Because of this, she has had the opportunity to play difficult and nuanced roles throughout her career, demonstrating her range as an actor and establishing her reputation as a reputable person in the field.

Furthermore, acknowledgment may also have a knock-on impact on the entertainment sector as a whole. When an actress like Natalie Portman receives recognition for her work, it encourages other young artists to follow their passions and aim for artistic perfection. This beneficial impact may help the entertainment sector as a whole to continue expanding and changing.

In conclusion, acknowledgment is important to the entertainment business and has a wide range of effects on the careers of performers like Natalie Portman. It affirms their ability, raises their profile in the industry, creates new prospects, and may even serve as an inspiration for the next artistic generations. Natalie Portman's career trajectory and that of others who follow in her footsteps will be shaped by the significance of notoriety in the entertainment business, which will not diminish as she pursues her professional goals.

Natalie Portman Giving Back via Charitable Events and Philanthropy

One of the most important aspects of Natalie Portman's life and profession is her dedication to philanthropic causes and events. She has continuously raised awareness and support for several issues using her platform as an actress, exhibiting a sincere commitment to having a beneficial influence on society.

Natalie Portman's main areas of interest are environmental protection. She has actively participated in spreading awareness of the effects of climate change and the significance of sustainable living as a supporter of animal rights and a vegan. She is one of the co-founders of the animal rights group Animal Equality, which aims to promote plant-based diets and put a stop to animal abuse. She has also worked with other groups to fight animal cruelty and advance veganism, including the Humane Society and People for the Ethical Treatment of Animals (PETA).

Portman's charitable endeavors go beyond protecting the environment. She has also actively supported a number of educational projects. She established the Natalie Portman Dance and Music Center in Jerusalem in 2006, providing theater, dance, and music instruction to children from low-income families. This program encourages creativity, self-expression, and personal development in addition to giving these kids the chance to showcase their abilities.

One noteworthy facet of Portman's philanthropic endeavors is her support of women's rights and empowerment. She has been a strong supporter of gender equality and has made use of her position to spread awareness of global problems impacting women. She was chosen in 2015 to be the first-ever Jewish woman to serve on the board of the Women's International Zionist Organization (WIZO), an organization that works to advance gender equality and social welfare in Israel, in its American branch.

Natalie Portman often takes part in different events and initiatives as part of her humanitarian activities. She has supported her chosen causes by attending a number of galas and fundraisers, including the Environmental Media Association Awards and the Humane Society's Genesis Awards. In addition, Portman has used her acting career to promote awareness in short films and documentaries. One such film is the 2009 documentary "Eating," which focuses on the negative effects of meat-eating on the environment.

Furthermore, a number of organizations have honored and acknowledged Portman's charitable endeavors. She was given the "Humanitarian of the Year" award by the Animal Rights National Conference in 2010 and the Animal Rights Award by PETA in 2015. These honors provide witness to her steadfast dedication to using her charitable endeavors to change the world.

In conclusion, one important facet of Natalie Portman's life and profession is her participation in philanthropic causes and events. Her commitment to women's rights, animal welfare, education, and environmental protection shows how passionate she is about utilizing her position to make a real difference in the world. Even if Portman's acting career takes off, her charitable work will surely always be a significant part of her legacy, encouraging people to give back and change the world.

CHAPTER 11

The Musical Adventures of Natalie

Singing and Acting in Stage and Motion Picture Productions

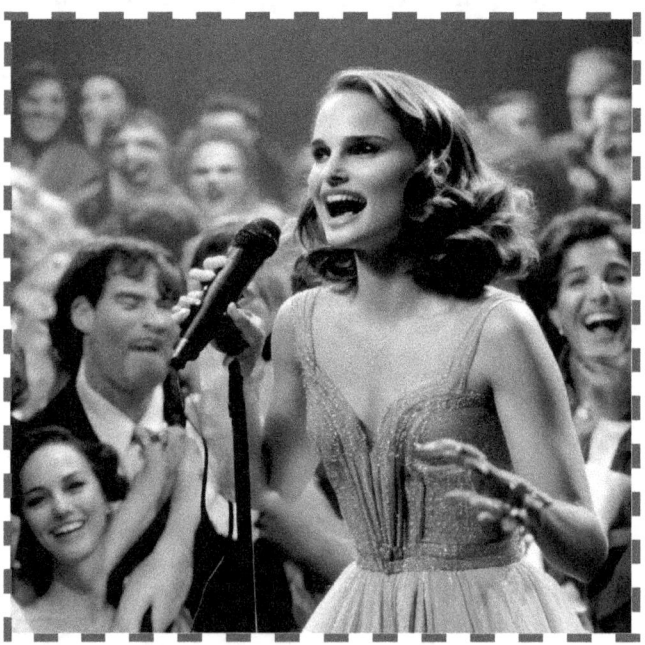

Natalie Portman has continuously shown off her diverse abilities when it comes to singing and acting in stage and cinema projects. She has been able to flourish in a variety of roles and captivate audiences with her engaging performances thanks to her wide skill set.

In the 1994 film "Léon: The Professional," Portman made her singing and performing debut in the French song "Désespérée," co-starring with actor Gary Oldman. This was one of her first public performances. Her future aspirations in the performing arts were paved with this early encounter.

Natalie Portman played the part of Evey Hammond in the dystopian film "V for Vendetta" in 2002. She had to sing the hymn "God Save the Queen," which she did well and with passion. She demonstrated her versatility as a musician throughout her performance.

In addition to her roles in movies, Natalie Portman has performed in a number of theatrical shows. Her Broadway debut was in a production of "The Seagull," which was directed by Mike Nichols, in 2008. Critics praised Portman's portrayal of the disturbed artist Nina, which cemented her status as a gifted stage actor.

Another noteworthy performance by Portman was in the Jean-Claude Carrière drama "The King of Egypt," which was produced in 2018. She played Queen Marie-Antoinette in this play, which required her to sing and provide strong performances that encapsulated the spirit of the historical personage.

Natalie Portman's portrayals of well-known artists have shown her vocal and performance abilities. In the 2014 biographical drama "Jane Got a Gun," she portrayed Jane, a singer; in the 2018 movie "Vox Lux," she played Celeste, a pop diva. By taking on these parts, Portman was able to broaden her performance repertoire and learn more about the difficulties and creative process experienced by musicians.

In addition, Portman's commitment to her work has allowed her to take on difficult parts requiring extraordinary vocal and performance abilities. She portrayed ballet ballerina Nina in the 2010 film "Black Swan," a role that required her to get intensive instruction in dance and deliver a performance that was very emotional. Her portrayal in this movie won her an Academy Award for Best Actress, demonstrating her extraordinary acting skills.

In summary, Natalie Portman's singing and acting roles in stage and movie performances have shown her extraordinary skill and flexibility. From her debut in "Léon: The Professional" to her most recent parts in "Vox Lux" and "The King of Egypt," Portman has continuously wowed audiences all around the globe with her mesmerizing performances. Her contributions to the singing community and her stage and cinema performances will undoubtedly inspire and enthrall audiences for years to come as she takes on new roles and challenges.

Working Together with Composers and Musicians

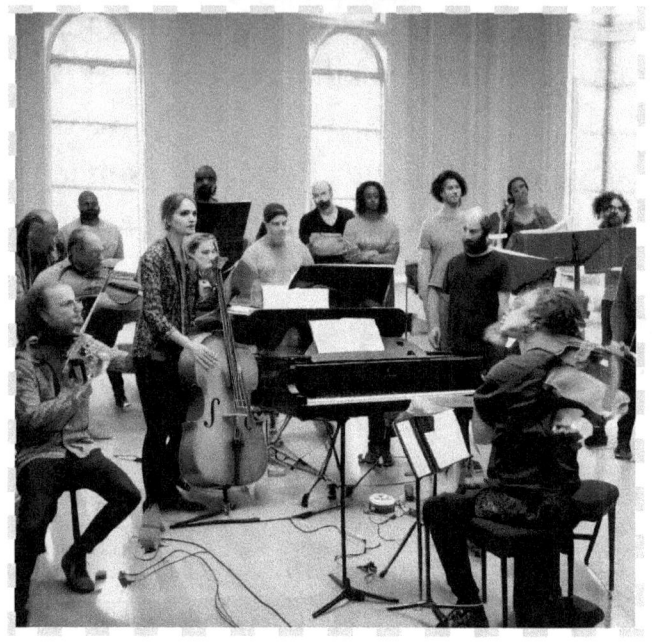

Natalie Portman and Musicians while Rehearsing

Natalie Portman's career has been diversified, with her partnerships with musicians and composers adding special musical components to her productions. These partnerships have given her the chance to not only experiment with other genres but also to develop a closer connection with the characters she plays.

In 1996, one of her first working relationships was with composer Michael Brook on the film "The Negotiator." Brook's eerie and atmospheric score enhanced the dramatic and suspenseful mood of the movie and laid the groundwork for Portman's subsequent partnerships with gifted musicians and composers.

Clint Mansell, a composer whose hauntingly beautiful music featured the Muse song "Stay," collaborated with Portman on the highly acclaimed film "V for Vendetta" in 2005. Mansell's work wonderfully fit the film's dark and dystopian themes. This partnership demonstrated Portman's capacity to collaborate with musicians of many genres, and the outcome was a powerful and enduring soundtrack.

Another noteworthy project was working with composer Alexandre Desplat on the 2010 movie "Black Swan." Desplat's dramatic soundtrack, which blended contemporary sounds with traditional ballet music, effectively portrayed the film's intensely emotional setting. Portman's portrayal as a ballet dancer in this movie strengthened her bond with the music and artistic communities.

For her cinematic ventures, Portman has worked with musicians in addition to composers. For example, she sang a French rendition of the song "Dream a Little Dream of Me" with singer-songwriter Sebastien Tellier in the 2006 movie "Paris, Je T'aime." Through this partnership, her repertoire as a performer was further expanded and she demonstrated her ability to adapt to numerous musical genres and languages.

Moreover, Portman's association with musicians and composers surpasses her involvement in cinema. She is a co-founder of Evolve Entertainment, a production business that specializes in film, television, and music-based content creation, which was established in 2015. By means of this endeavor, Portman has persisted in working with diverse musicians, therefore strengthening her dedication to the realm of music and entertainment.

Working with musicians and composers has improved Natalie Portman's film ventures and opened up new creative possibilities for her. Her contributions to the film and music industries will undoubtedly inspire and enthrall viewers for years to come as long as she keeps working with gifted musicians from a variety of musical backgrounds.

Natalie Portman's Passion for Music and How It Affected Her Professional Life

Natalie Portman's career, both on and off screen, has been greatly influenced by her love of music. This interest has impacted her decisions for personal and cinematic projects, in addition to leading her to work with a variety of artists and composers.

Natalie Portman's parents, who were also artists, introduced her to music at a young age. She was raised with a strong awareness for a wide range of musical genres and styles by her mother, an American artist and housewife, and father, an Israeli-born writer. Early exposure to a wide range of musical styles will subsequently have a significant effect on her career.

Recognizing the value of music in bringing her film projects to life on a deeper emotional level, Portman started looking for chances to collaborate with musicians and composers as her acting career took off. Her commitment to using music in her films prompted her to engage with a variety of gifted musicians, each of whom contributed their own musical viewpoints.

Her performance in the 2006 anthology film "Paris, Je T'aime," in which she costarred with singer-songwriter Sebastien Tellier and sang a French rendition of the beloved song "Dream a Little Dream of Me," is among the most noteworthy instances of Portman's passion for music impacting her career. Her flexibility as an artist and her openness to trying out different creative directions were shown by this encounter.

Natalie Portman's love of music has permeated every aspect of her daily existence. She is a talented pianist who has been seen to play for fun and pleasure. She has also mentioned how much she loves a variety of musical styles, such as indie rock, jazz, and classical. Her selections for film projects have surely been impacted by her broad taste of music, since she is attracted to storylines that include or center around music.

Apart from her work in front of the camera, Portman has collaborated on projects fusing music, cinema, and television. She is one of the co-founders of the production business Evolve Entertainment, which specializes in combining several creative genres to create entertainment. By pursuing this endeavor, Portman shows how much her passion for music has influenced her work and how she is still exploring the connections between music and cinema.

In conclusion, Natalie Portman's passion for music has fueled both her professional and personal achievements. Her love of several musical genres has inspired her to work with outstanding musicians and composers on noteworthy cinema projects. Furthermore, she has been motivated to produce work that highlights the potency of both two forms when united by her commitment to investigating the relationships between music and cinema. Her passion for music will surely always be a driving factor in Portman's career, impacting her work and providing inspiration for upcoming musicians.

Her Life's Intersection of Acting and Music

Natalie Portman's career has benefited greatly from the convergence of her passions for acting and music, which enhances her performances and creative pursuits. She has continuously looked for chances to investigate the relationships between these two creative disciplines throughout her career as an artist, producing a body of work that is both inspirational and varied.

Early exposure to a variety of musical genres and styles by her artistically interested parents led to Portman's early love of music. Her early love of music would eventually inform her decisions about upcoming motion pictures and serve as motivation for her partnerships with musicians and composers.

Her performance in the 2006 anthology film "Paris, Je T'aime," in which she co-starred with singer-songwriter Sebastien Tellier on a French rendition of the beloved song "Dream a Little Dream of Me," is among the most noteworthy instances of Portman's lifelong connection between acting and music. Her flexibility as an artist and her openness to trying out different creative directions were shown by this encounter.

Apart from her work in front of the camera, Portman has collaborated on projects fusing music, cinema, and television. She is one of the co-founders of the production business Evolve Entertainment, which specializes in combining several creative genres to create entertainment. By pursuing this endeavor, Portman shows how much her passion for music has influenced her work and how she is still exploring the connections between acting and music.

Natalie Portman's acting endeavors have also benefited greatly from her partnerships with songwriters and musicians. Her collaboration with composer Alexandre Desplat, for example, produced an evocative music for the 2010 picture "Black Swan" that flawlessly portrayed the film's deep emotional environment. This partnership demonstrated how acting and music may work together to provide a more meaningful and lasting cinematic experience.

In addition, Portman's passion for music has shaped the films she has chosen to work on. She enjoys reading books that include music because it gives her an opportunity to investigate the relationships between these two creative forms. Her commitment to investigating the relationship between acting and music has allowed her to work on films like "Cold Mountain," "Where the Heart Is," and "The Professional," where music was an important part of the story.

Natalie Portman's successful professional and personal pursuits have been fueled by the convergence of her passions for acting and music. Her love of many musical genres and her commitment to investigating the relationship between acting and music have allowed her to work with exceptional musicians on some very remarkable cinematic productions. Her passion for music will surely always be a driving factor in Portman's professional life, prompting her to produce material that highlights the potency of both two genres when united.

Discovering Novel Creative Channels and Interests

A key component of Natalie Portman's development both personal and professional has been her commitment to discovering new creative outlets and hobbies. In her artistic career, she has always looked for ways to broaden her horizons and experiment with other kinds of expression.

Her work in academics is one of the most noteworthy instances of Portman's search for new creative opportunities. She went after her studies with great enthusiasm, graduating from Harvard University with a bachelor's degree in psychology and the Hebrew University of Jerusalem with a doctorate in the same field. Her comprehension of human behavior has been enhanced by her academic journey, which has also enabled her to investigate the nexus between psychology and the arts, thus intensifying her artistic interests.

Apart from her educational endeavors, Portman has been a supporter of environmental concerns and animal rights. She was a co-founder of The Animal Compassion Foundation, an animal rights group that subsequently evolved into Noble, a vegan footwear brand. She was able to demonstrate her business spirit and explore her interest for activism and the environment via this endeavor.

Portman's dedication to investigating new artistic mediums has permeated her filmography as well. She has accepted parts that test her abilities as an actor and let her explore a wide range of people and narratives. A case in point is her performance as Jacqueline Kennedy in the 2016 motion picture "Jackie," which necessitated her complete submersion into the realms of politics, history, and mourning. Her ability to inhabit many personalities was shown in this part, underscoring her commitment to broadening her acting repertoire.

Directing is another example of Portman's search for new creative avenues. In 2019, she directed her first short film, "Eve," for which she also wrote and acted. She was able to learn more about the creative process behind the camera with this project, which enhanced her knowledge of narrative and filmmaking.

In addition, Portman's passion for dancing has influenced both her personal and professional life. She's trained in ballroom, salsa, and ballet, among other dance forms. Her commitment to dance has given her a special creative outlet in addition to improving her acting skills. Her love of dancing brought her to the big screen in the 2010 film "Black Swan," where she played a ballet ballerina and showed off her incredible emotional and physical metamorphosis.

In summary, Natalie Portman's success in her work and personal development may be attributed to her dedication to discovering new interests and creative outlets. Her wide range of interests and activities has made it possible for her to express herself creatively in a variety of ways, producing a body of work that is both rich and varied. Her commitment to exploring fresh artistic directions will surely continue to be a driving factor as Portman develops as an artist, encouraging her to produce and make contributions that improve both her life and the lives of others.

Moral Lessons from Natalie Portman's Life and Career

Many moral lessons that encourage and mentor people to follow their interests, uphold integrity, and aim for greatness may be drawn from Natalie Portman's life and work. Some of these important lessons are highlighted in the list below, along with a brief explanation of their importance:

❖ *Accept a variety of interests and hobbies:* Natalie Portman has continuously looked for new artistic endeavors and passions throughout her career, including dance, activism, and education. This openness to experimenting with many subjects highlights the value of pursuing one's passions and never stopping learning, both of which may result in personal development and a more contented existence.

❖ The importance of aiming for greatness in one's chosen sector is shown by Portman's commitment to her acting career, as well as her scholarly and activist endeavors. The end product of this dedication to mastery is not just outstanding work, but it also inspires others to realize their own potential.

❖ *Stand up for what you believe in:* Natalie Portman has made no secret of her support for a number of issues, including environmental preservation and animal rights. Her action serves as a reminder of how important it is to defend one's morals and convictions, especially in the face of difficulty or opposition. The importance of utilizing one's platform and power to bring about good change in the world is emphasized by this moral lesson.

❖ *Maintain a healthy balance between your personal and professional life:* Portman's devotion to her family and personal life, together with her successful job, highlights the significance of doing so. This lesson urges people to put their relationships and well-being first so they don't let their job overtake them.

❖ *Always learn and adjust:* Natalie Portman is a great example of the need of constant learning and adaptation, as shown by her academic endeavors and openness to trying out new artistic endeavors. This moral lesson underscores the need of maintaining an open mind, adjusting to new circumstances, and welcoming personal development throughout one's lifetime.

❖ *Respect and assist others:* Portman exemplifies the value of appreciating and assisting others in their endeavors by her collaborative approach to her work and her support of other artists, activists, and scholars. In order to support those around them in their pursuit of achievement and personal development, this lesson urges people to cultivate a feeling of community and collaboration.

- ❖ ***Remain modest and grounded:*** Natalie Portman maintains her modesty and groundedness in the face of her success, attributing it to the help and direction of others. This moral lesson emphasizes the need of keeping an attitude of appreciation and realizing that many people work together to achieve success.

In Summary, Natalie Portman's life and profession provide insightful moral teachings that may uplift and mentor people in a variety of spheres of their lives. People may carve out their own pathways to success and personal satisfaction by accepting a variety of interests, aiming for excellence, sticking to one's convictions, juggling their personal and professional lives, never stopping learning, showing respect for and helping others, and maintaining their humility.

CONCLUSION

In conclusion this biography book "A Star's Sacrifice: Unleashing Natalie Portman's Extraordinary Life and Career in Hollywood - A Tale of Commitment and Great Dedication" is very inspirational, detailing her rise from a young actress to a renowned actor and respected scholar. Her exceptional skill, unwavering devotion to her art, and support of social and environmental concerns have made her a significant figure in the entertainment sector and beyond. Portman's accomplishments in both performing and education demonstrate her versatility and her unwavering commitment to perfection serves as an example for young artists and activists everywhere.